RELOADED

<small>AN</small>
AMERICAN

WARNING

SUBCOMPACT EDITION

SAME GREAT CONTENT – SMALLER SIZE

RELOADED

AN AMERICAN

WARNING

SUBCOMPACT EDITION

DAVID M ROBERTSON

ANOTHER

PUBLICATION

Second Edition: August 2017
10 9 8 7 6 5 4 3 2

ISBN-13: 978-0692930991
ISBN-10: 069293099X

RELOADED: An American Warning – SubCompact Edition / David M Robertson
Cover design © 2014 - 2017 David M Robertson. All rights reserved.

The views expressed in this work are solely those of the author.

Originally Published with AuthorHouse™ LLC
© 2014 David M.Robertson. All rights reserved.
Library of Congress Control Number: 2013923748

NOTE: This work has been lightly re-edited for quality purposes but the content overall has remained the same.

"To our Founding Fathers who gave us everything we take for granted and to our children who will inherit the mess we give them"

David M Robertson

TABLE OF CONTENTS

WARNING

According to the federal government, you may now be suspect as a domestic terror threat for having acquired, read and/or subscribing to the information in this book. This is especially true if you are a former law enforcement officer or veteran of the armed forces of the United States.

As provided by the Department of Homeland Security (DHS), namely the Transportation Security Administration (TSA) and Federal Emergency Management Agency (FEMA), if you subscribe to and/or possess any of the following, you may be considered a domestic terror threat:

- Expressions of libertarian philosophies (statements, bumper stickers)
- Second Amendment-oriented views (NRA or holding a CCW permit)
- Possess Survivalist literature or subscribe to Survivalist Blogs
- Self-sufficiency (stockpiling food, ammo, hand tools, medical supplies)
- Fear of economic collapse (buying gold and barter items)

- Expressed fears of Big Brother or big government
- Homeschooling
- Declarations of Constitutional rights and civil liberties
- Belief in a New World Order conspiracy
- Support to a third party or third party candidate—
  (Rawles, 2012)

The information provided within will not be fun to read. There are times that you will find yourself uncomfortable with the information and what the information ultimately means to you and your family. There will be times when you will feel overwhelmed with what you are reading as you reflect on what you already know and as you discover undeniable truth.

Consider this book your "*Truth 101*" textbook. We must discover the true threat and fundamentally understand that we are all in this together. Our country is in trouble.

Lines are being drawn against you daily. There are those who THINK they support and defend the Constitution, and are those who really do support and defend the Constitution. Then, there are those in the middle who simply have no idea whatsoever. By the time you are finished with this book, you will know where you stand.

Ignorance is public enemy number one. I challenge you to read this book in its entirety with an open mind. By doing so, you will be better equipped to consider all sides of the issue and choose your side accordingly.

This book will challenge you. This book will change you. Remember, being smart and having information is a good thing. This is An American Warning. Will you heed it?

AN AMERICAN WARNING

Introduction

Undoubtedly, you already know that something is severely wrong in our great nation, or you have heard that things are messed up and you are curious about some of the issues we face. Maybe, a friend recommended the book because they value you as an intellectual and hope you will find value within these pages. Regardless, by taking the step to acquire and read this book, you have shown initiative. You undoubtedly hold leadership abilities within your character profile. This is important to note because all leaders must understand where they will lead others and for what reasons.

If you have even a mild awareness of the condition our nation is in, you have probably wondered what many others have pondered, "*How did we get here and what can we do to fix it?*" You must understand that you are not alone in your thoughts or in the struggle.

You are going to read about many of the problems that we face as a nation, in simple, easy to understand terms and without partisan blinders. Every single chapter in this book is connected to the one before it and each will undoubtedly challenge what you currently believe or understand.

This book will present ideas that will be difficult for some to accept. You may not have heard of some of what you will discover. This is because the propaganda and government-run education has already taken its toll on most. That does not make the reality any less true or any less dire.

In this book, we throw partisan politics to the wind and focus on the foundation of the problem. By doing so, we self-analyze because undoubtedly we have all played a part in the bigger problem. We are all to blame in some way shape or form. For example: while you may not have passed the legislation, you have followed, enforced, and taught others that such legislation is okay to follow.

This book is not about Left or Right, it is about our future. This book is about you. It is about us. You should find yourself evaluating your own beliefs and perhaps how you have contributed to the problem, as well as examining how you can help fix it.

The two primary parties have been way too wrong for far too long, and because of this, our great nation appears as though it is about to come to a sudden and probably violent end. It will happen the same way that every other nation with a corrupt and bankrupt government has ended, tragically and completely avoidable.

Right now it is imperative that everyone realize what is really happening to us. We must get over this left-right, Democrat- Republican lie we have all been sold and realize our place in the world. We have been divided in order to be conquered.

This will not be a sugar-coated journey through fiction. This is as real as it gets and you should know that our situation is going to get worse long before it gets better. If you care at all about your country and want to see the madness cease, take some time to read this now—while you can. Do not procrastinate.

This book is intended to give you some basic resources to question everything with boldness. It is not designed to give you the *"in's and out's"* of every single topic. There is no way that I could cover everything in extreme depth. So do not take the words in this book as the *"end-all"* to any debate or position. Research and find the truth, connect the dots, get informed, and make up your own mind.

The purpose of this book is to empower you with perspectives that are not readily available or taught at this time. There will also be a list of additional resources that you are highly encouraged to review.

Finally, try to understand that this book has been written with the intent to allow people from all education levels and backgrounds to easily accept and interpret the information. Some of the concepts are simplified for a specific reason. It would be unwise and downright counterproductive to provide a book that few could either read or understand. We are all in this together whether or not we like it or even know it. The hope is that at the very least, you will walk away from this book better equipped to research further.

I love my country, but we must examine it with an honest eye. We cannot allow our love of country to blind us from truth. If we continue to lie to ourselves, we will never be able to address the issues that we truly face.

In the future, this book will be a good example of how some saw, some tried, but many either ignored or refused to see. By the time you finish this book, you will no longer be able to say that you were not warned.

With these things in mind . . . sit back, relax, and let us start the journey!

Part 1 – Foundation Decay

The Republic

For generations, the American people have heard it said in schools, they have read it in books, read it in pop-culture magazines and heard it on television. It has been the battle cry for military action and the reason to endure hardships faced by the citizenry. The term "Democracy" has become synonymous with the United States of America. Did you know that this is an inaccurate description of what we are? More accurately asked: did you know that it is a horrible and most terrible lie?

Dr. James McHenry, one of Maryland's delegates to the Constitutional Convention of 1787, had his notes published in The American Historical Review, vol. 11, 1906. His anecdote on page 618 reads: "*A lady asked Dr. Franklin* (Benjamin Franklin) "*Well Doctor what have we got a republic or a monarchy?*" "*A republic . . .*" replied the Doctor "*. . . if you can keep it*" (McHenry, 1906). As a matter of fact, the idea of the Republic was actually solidified in our very own Constitution.

Article 4 Section 4 of the United States Constitution states clearly that "*The United States shall guarantee to every state in this union a republican form of government, and shall protect each of them against invasion; . . .*" (US Const.)

This is not meant to insinuate that the Republican Party is to be in control of each state. Actually, that statement has nothing to do with the Republican Party whatsoever.

The first question you need to ask yourself is exactly why or how so many of the *"Constitutional Scholars"* who pretend to be leading us, have missed this crucial and fundamental point within the text of the Constitution?

By definition, a Republic is *"a state in which supreme power is held by the people and their elected representatives, and which has an elected or nominated president rather than a monarch"* (Republic, n.d.). So why the confusion?

By definition, a Democracy is *"a form of government in which people choose leaders by voting"*. (Democracy, n.d.)

If you ponder this long enough, you will begin to see the disconnection. When you research further, you will begin to see that in a Republic, everyone is equal and citizens are born with the right to participate in government, electing representatives to exercise power on behalf of the people.

In a Democracy, people are NOT equal and citizens are granted permission to participate by the government, electing leaders to make decisions for them. This is a massive disconnect and something that is often not taught in schools. Can you see the problem with this?

It could be argued that this problem began with the 32nd U.S. President, Mr. Franklin D. Roosevelt and his *"New Deal"* which history has shown to be a very bad deal. The best retort for the inevitable question of *"why?"* is that the road to hell is often paved with the best of intentions.

The New Deal fundamentally destroyed the Republic because it eradicated the possibility of equality, it established the entitlement system, and placed government at the center of the power paradigm. Essentially, FDR ruined the foundation of America, he did not save it. He transformed it. This should have been self-evident for most Americans but history has been blinded by the events of that time such as the Great Depression and World War II, of which FDR was President during.

This is similar to how Rudy Giuliani, then Mayor of New York City, was somehow given a pass for his less than adequate abilities to govern and his bad policies due to the horrible events of September 11th, 2001 (Kellerman, 2004). The tragedy faced by a nation should not and does not change the facts surrounding a leader's "rule".

This is undoubtedly a bold claim that contradicts much of what you have probably learned in school. Yes, these are merely opinions but they are opinions based on what history has shown to us. My intent is not to bash specific leaders or their abilities per say. It is to point out the truth. Hind sight is indeed 20/20, but should we not course correct understanding now just how bad things have become?

Of course, there are those who could argue that our decline began with Woodrow Wilson. This is a valid debate, and I can concede to the idea that at the very minimum, Wilson laid the groundwork for the actual attack by FDR. Either way, together their *"policies"* fundamentally destroyed what our founders wanted.

The basic idea of this chapter is to understand that in order to repair what has been broken, we must first figure out exactly what has been broken and what it means to the overall foundation.

We have to understand and agree that equal liberty requires that no one has the right to rule another without that other's consent. The Republic is freedom. The Republic is true equality. The Republic is power in the hands of the people. The Republic is a reduction or elimination of the perceived and actually received tyranny, more than anything though, the Republic allows for self- reliance and self-responsibility.

Yes, there are many in this great nation who no longer respect or want the Republic, but this childish position does not negate the intent of what was fought and died for by the founders, nor does it negate the responsibility to ensure its place for future generations. We are NOT a Democracy.

There are those who would call us a Christian nation as well. Sure, roughly 70% of the people in this nation are Christian, but over 50% of the population is female, and over 50% of the workforce is female, does that mean we are a *"Feminine Nation"*? Of course not.

Furthering that point, one would have to ask exactly which sect of Christianity would we be exactly if we were a Christian nation? Quaker, Catholic, Protestant, Calvinist, etc.? This idea just seems silly considering that many of the writers of our founding documents were Deist or Unitarian. Of course, this is probably the first time many of you have heard such a notion and that is okay. This will be one of many revelations during your reading.

Benjamin Franklin, Ethan Allen, George Washington, James Madison, John Locke, Thomas Paine, Thomas Jefferson, etc. Things are not always as they appear.

It just helps to know about the foundation in order to build upon it.

The Declaration of Independence (The Part They Don't Teach)

Everyone knows deep down inside, that each of us is created equal, and that their God (whomever that might be) has given them certain fundamental rights belonging to everyone, which cannot be taken away no matter what. These Rights are Life, Liberty and the pursuit of Happiness.—and to make sure these rights are always there, Governments are established alongside the people, created by the people, for the people, and the government's powers are given to them with consent by the people they govern,—And whenever any form of government becomes destructive, abusive, or overbearing, it is the Right of the People to change it or over throw it, and to establish new Government in its place, laying its foundation on these principles and organizing its powers in this form, to make sure they continue to have Safety and Happiness. Of course discretion should be used in these matters, and Governments that have been around for a long time should not be overthrown or challenged for trivial reasons; however history has shown that mankind is more apt to suffer through unnecessary burdens that hinder these rights than to fix the problems by getting rid of or getting out of the situations they are suffering from. So when a long list of abuses and violations continue to grow, it becomes clear that the people should get out from underneath this total dictatorship. It is their right, it is their duty, to separate themselves from such Government, for nothing more than to make sure their future is secure.—This has been the problem; and because of this, we choose to create a new government unlike the government we are currently under. This government has a history of repeated abuses and violations, providing nothing more than total dictatorship over these States.

Perhaps you might have heard something like this before? What you have just read is a modern translation of the Preamble to the Declaration of Independence. Many find the preceding to be absolutely remarkable because it sounds much like the cries of citizens across this great nation almost weekly anymore; cries from the left, right, rich and poor, cries very similar to that of our Founding Fathers more than 200 years ago. Still, so many people today do not know a thing about this very important document. How does this happen?

The Declaration of Independence was written by our Founding Fathers because they realized that their King (government) would not listen to them and did not care what they had to say. Their "*Central Bank*" far surpassed its acceptable boundaries, and the government was reaping great benefits from the labors of the colonists without any substantial gain to the colonists in return.

At first and primarily out of loyalty, the colonists accepted the hardships and higher taxes imposed on them. Though, as time went on, the colonists began to see that they were being treated more like work horses rather than valued colonists. The hard work and constant danger was bad enough without a having a tyrant half a world away stealing from the tables of those who risked it all to acquire what they had.

Still, the colonists thrived for a time and the more they thrived, the more the King took. This pattern proceeded to get worse over time. It elevated to such a degree that when the people would ask for something, the establishment simply would not listen. Instead, the king invaded the people's privacy and created many new government programs that were enforced by intimidation. For his personal use, the king took property and money away from almost everyone. The King then established numerous laws that restricted or banned the tools necessary for self-protection. Of course this was a major issue.

Much like today, this tyranny was accepted by the people primarily out of loyalty, but reinforced through official sounding declarations such as the American Revenue Act (Sugar Tax), Boston Port Act, the Massachusetts Government Act, and the Quartering Act which were also known as the "*Intolerable Acts*".

You might remember how the officials enforced something known as the tax stamp which taxed every piece of printed material including playing cards. More or less, these were all attempts to create more burdens on the people so that in turn, they would be forced to rely on the government more and follow what the government said.

Our Founding Fathers tried numerous times to plea with the King to allow them an opportunity to right some of these wrongs. Our Founding Fathers wanted government representation by fellow citizens from the colonies, not by people halfway around the world. The representatives they were provided were people who knew nothing about life in the colonies. They were too far detached.

The colonists considered the provided representatives to be elitists. It was understood that these *"representatives"* were not common and did not care about the hardships of those in the proverbial trenches. So, when certain laws were passed and abuses to those laws were exercised, the hardships that were imposed on the people went unchecked and the cries of the people were left unheard.

Is this not our situation today at least in part? Can you imagine a government that did what it wanted to do without citizen oversight? Can you imagine officials of that government not listening to the vast majority of the people? Can you imagine officials that only wanted to further advance the power of the government or themselves and were willing to lie, cheat, and steal to do it? Can you imagine elitists representing you who were detached, knowing nothing about you or your hardships, or what life is like in your community?

If you are saying to yourself that this all sounds too familiar, understand that you are not alone. It sounds surprisingly familiar because it is. You are in very similar shoes to that of our founders. Understand though, that over a long enough period of time; they decided they were going to do something about it.

It was not an immediate call to arms though. As stated earlier, they did try to plea with the king and the kings' officials. They tried numerous letters, numerous visits with officials, and persistent patience with the hardships they were dealing with every day. After all, they were loyal to Britain and they just wanted to advance the empire.

They did however feel as though they deserved perhaps just a little in exchange for their bravery and hard work. They did not ask for much either. They simply wanted to be left alone and have the ability to be self-reliant. The king and his officials did not see these as great options because they wanted to advance their own agendas. The truth was that the people were nothing more than the work horses to make that happen. Slowly, the people caught on.

The colonists worked hard to acquire resources but found that they were not being justly compensated for their work. Many of resources found or harvested were more or less confiscated for the crown and were sent straight back to England. Much of the territory the colonists were trying to settle was taken away by the lords, and the colonists were told they could not push further west. They were forced to stay right where they were in many cases. They began to see that their dreams were fading, and for what?

When the kings' soldiers began to enforce many of the kings' unreasonable demands, the people started to consider a separation from Britain. After all, the king was not listening anymore, the kings' officials would not pay attention to the people, and the fact that the people were working more for their "*government*" than they were for their own livelihoods had just become too much.

The colonists believed they were living in a complete dictatorship, only this dictatorship was known as a monarchy. Eventually, and after volunteering to come to this new land and taking enormous risks, the colonists did not feel that having their property or lives controlled by another was right. They knew what they were experiencing was fundamentally wrong, and they needed to do something about it. A change was soon to come.

Our Founding Fathers soon wrote one of the most amazing documents ever created. Because of this document, a chain of events ensued that eventually birthed the greatest nation the world had ever seen. As Americans, we have a responsibility to remember with a patriotic heart, all of those freedoms they fought so hard to provide every citizen of the United States of America. Not just the freedoms though, we should remember the reasons.

We should acknowledge and embrace the words and ideals of our Founding Fathers when it comes to our freedoms and livelihoods. We should not try to "*fix*" or "*re-create*" America, we should be holding on to what we were told would keep our freedoms intact. Remember; the type of liberty we are supposed to have (the Republic) is a fairly unpopular idea because it empowers everyone equally, and those who have power seldom like to share it. This idea still holds true today.

Let us examine the reasons addressed in the Declaration of Independence and provide some context in modern terms so as to better understand where they were coming from. Note that when the term "*He*" is used, they were referring to the King.

He has refused his Assent to Laws, the most wholesome and necessary for the public good.—*The King refused to agree to wholesome and necessary laws that the colonists requested.*

He has forbidden his Governors to pass Laws of immediate and pressing importance, unless suspended in their operation till his Assent should be obtained; and when so suspended, he has utterly neglected to attend to them.—*The King refused to let the Governors permission to pass laws without the approval of each and every law regardless of their necessity or importance and often ignored some requests all together.*

He has refused to pass other Laws for the accommodation of large districts of people, unless those people would relinquish the right of Representation in the Legislature, a right inestimable to them and formidable to tyrants only.—*The King would only grant accommodation if the people gave up their rights to participate in their local governments.*

He has called together legislative bodies at places unusual, uncomfortable, and distant from the depository of their public Records, for the sole purpose of fatiguing them into compliance with his measures.—*The King deliberately made it difficult for the people to participate in or even observe government proceedings that involved them directly. IE: behind closed doors.*

He has dissolved Representative Houses repeatedly, for opposing with manly firmness his invasions on the rights of the people.—*The King dissolved representative bodies of the colonies for various reasons.*

He has refused for a long time, after such dissolutions, to cause others to be elected; whereby the Legislative powers, incapable of Annihilation, have returned to the People at large for their exercise; the State remaining in the mean time exposed to all the dangers of invasion from without, and convulsions within.—*After the King dissolved the representative bodies, he would not allow the people to form new bodies even when it was necessary for the safety and protection of the people. Essentially, the Right to be able to defend themselves was taken away.*

He has endeavored to prevent the population of these States; for that purpose obstructing the Laws for Naturalization of Foreigners; refusing to pass others to encourage their migrations hither, and raising the conditions of new Appropriations of Lands.—*The King restricted the migration of people to the states in an effort to keep them weak and reliant. He made all kinds of rules and laws that contorted the process.*

He has obstructed the Administration of Justice, by refusing his Assent to Laws for establishing Judiciary powers.—*Some areas had to go without a court of law for a long period of time because the English objected to the idea of anyone but the King having such power.*

He has made Judges dependent on his Will alone, for the tenure of their offices, and the amount and payment of their salaries.—*This was more than likely the inspiration for Article III, Section 1 of the United States Constitution.*

He has erected a multitude of New Offices, and sent hither swarms of Officers to harass our people, and eat out their substance.—*Imagine customs agents, TSA, NSA, IRS, military courts, etc. Agencies put in place by the government but without the consent of the colonists or the colonial legislatures.*

He has kept among us, in times of peace, Standing Armies without the Consent of our legislatures.—*A military force among the people at all times was/is unacceptable if it is not approved by the people.*

He has affected to render the Military independent of and superior to the Civil power.—*He has made the military power stronger than our system of justice, and they impose their will accordingly.*

He has combined with others to subject us to a jurisdiction foreign to our constitution, and unacknowledged by our laws; giving his Assent to their Acts of pretended Legislation:—*He has teamed up with other forces and we have to follow all kinds of rules and he does not even want to hear our own laws and what we think should be done.*

For quartering large bodies of armed troops among us:—*We have to house and feed complete strangers who are here to oppress us.*

For protecting them, by a mock Trial, from punishment for any Murders which they should commit on the Inhabitants of these States:—*He protects these people when they kill our people for no reason in so called trials.*

For cutting off our Trade with all parts of the world:—*He stopped us from trading with others.*

For imposing Taxes on us without our Consent:—*He continues to raise taxes without even asking us.*

For depriving us in many cases, of the benefits of Trial by Jury:—*He has taken away our Right to trial by jury in many cases.*

For transporting us beyond Seas to be tried for pretended offences—*He kidnaps us to be tried for charges that are ridiculous.*

For abolishing the free System of English Laws in a neighboring Province, establishing therein an Arbitrary government, and enlarging its Boundaries so as to render it at once an example and fit instrument for introducing the same absolute rule into these Colonies:—*More or less, this refers to rendering established laws obsolete, expanding the rule of the King, forcing his own laws on the people and making an example of those who do not follow.*

For taking away our Charters, abolishing our most valuable Laws, and altering fundamentally the Forms of our Governments - *He has taken away our ability to govern ourselves.*

For suspending our own Legislatures, and declaring themselves invested with power to legislate for us in all cases whatsoever.—*Rendering our laws moot, and forcing us to follow other laws.*

He has abdicated Government here, by declaring us out of his Protection and waging War against us.—*He abolished our government, disowned us, will not allow us to protect ourselves and he will not protect us either, and threatened war against us.*

He has plundered our seas, ravaged our Coasts, burnt our towns, and destroyed the lives of our people.—*He has taken our resources, burned our towns, and devastated so many people here.*

He is at this time transporting large Armies of foreign Mercenaries to complete the work s of death, desolation and tyranny, already begun with circumstances of Cruelty & perfidy scarcely paralleled in the most barbarous ages, and totally unworthy the Head of a civilized nation.—*From what we understand, he is sending Germans Mercenaries to come kill us, destroy what we have built, and make us a memory. This is not civilized behavior.*

He has constrained our fellow Citizens taken Captive on the high Seas to bear Arms against their Country, to become the executioners of their friends and Brethren, or to fall themselves by their Hands.—*When he has captured our brothers and sisters at sea, he has forced their service to take arms against us.*

He has excited domestic insurrections amongst us, and has endeavored to bring on the inhabitants of our frontiers, the merciless Indian Savages, whose known rule of warfare, is an undistinguished destruction of all ages, sexes and conditions.—*He has turned colonists against one another and had invited the Indians to come battle with us. These people do not fight like English people.*

(U.S. Declaration of Independence, 1776)

You might recall parts of this from when you were in grade school. It is often forgotten by most though and by the time it becomes a crucial thing to know, people have long since forgotten the details while yet others simply consider it all *"elementary"*. Still, one might find it interesting to know that we can actually draw some parallels between then and now.

Has the government in anyway shape or form, hindered our safety or national security for what appear to be dumb reasons?— Think Operation Gun Runner or Operation Fast and Furious. Has the government attempted to stop the states from passing what the states believe to be reasonable and needed laws?—Think about laws such as the Second Amendment Protection Act in at least 37 states and how the feds are threatening governors for attempting to pass such laws.

Has the government provided accommodations for certain states or companies if the people of those groups gave up any of their rights to participate in the program?—Think entitlements. Has the government had proceedings behind closed doors where the people were not allowed to hear or perhaps even the press was not allowed?—Think the Trans Pacific Partnership (among many others).

Has the government effectively stopped representative parties from being formed at all?—Think third parties or bodies held for grievances. Has government contorted the immigration rules to make it difficult for someone who wants to be a citizen for the right reasons to actually achieve citizenship?—Think Legal vs Criminal Immigrant.

Has government stopped or hindered a state's ability to protect itself?—Think Arizona. Has the federal government tried to establish its power over the states? Has it attempted to put itself above the states? Has the government become a revolving door with corrupt organizations?

Has the government created a multitude of agencies whose entire purpose seems to be harassing the people of this great nation if they are somehow affiliated with anything remotely close to something Constitution oriented?—Think TSA, NSA, IRS, etc.

Are we seeing military more and more often? Do we have a militarized police force? Is military equipment being utilized as normal everyday equipment? Is the government signing treaties that infringe on our fundamental Constitutional Rights?—Think UN Small Arms Treaty.

If a government official does something that ends up in the death of an American citizen, is that person brought to trial or is that person protected by the Administration?—Plenty of examples here but for those who are not aware please reference Clinton/ Benghazi or Holder/Gun Runner.

Are taxes continuing to be raised without consent? Are we fined for not paying? Can they be fined for being late with a payment to you? What about your trial by jury or being kidnapped to answer for crazy charges without Due Process?—Think National Defense Authorization Act

Is the government growing its own power and trying to render the self-rule a thing of the past?—Try to think about all the different areas of your life the government is actually in. Are any federal laws somehow infringing on Constitutional Rights or laws? Can you govern yourself?

Has the government threatened war against its people?—Think DHS in conjunction with the MIAC Report of 2009, or the Virginia Terrorism Threat Assessment 2009 which states that third party supporters, Ron Paul supporters, even Constitution loving Americans, were all domestic terror threats.

Has your government turned people on one another? Has the government forced Americans to point their guns at other Americans?—Think Katrina Gun Confiscations, think Boston, etc.

With the exception of a few listings, we have just drawn a parallel to the entirety of the Declaration of Independence. In almost every single category, there are examples of similar problems that our founders faced. In fact, some of you are looking at the examples provided and you are ridiculing them because you can come up with far better examples that illustrate the point much more effectively. This only furthers the point. If you can find better examples for these, you are already making the case. It is a simple point. We are pretty much where our founders were; only this beast has gotten bigger, stronger, and more resolute. Are you amazed more people do not see this?

The Constitution – An Idea

The Constitution is an idea. It is the aim or purpose for these great United States. It is also a very short document. As originally written and ratified, the Constitution of the United States consists of 4618 words (including signatures) arranged into seven articles. There have been 27 amendments to the original document, not all of them exactly favorites of the people.

The Constitution of the United States is NOT some long involved document such as the Patriot Act, the Tax Code, or even the Affordable Care Act. If you want to look at it realistically, by comparison, a short story is 2,500 to 5,000 words and approximately 10 to 20 pages long.

The responsibility for every American to read and understand the Constitution and the Bill of Rights should be fundamental. Sure, it was covered in grade school, but do you remember it? Do you know it?

This is VITAL to contemplate because there are some in our great nation who are tasked with protecting our Constitution. In fact, at the time of this entry, there are over 800,000 law enforcement personnel and over 1,450,000 military personnel who have all swore an oath to uphold and defend the Constitution against all enemies both foreign and domestic. In fact, explore this idea for a moment.

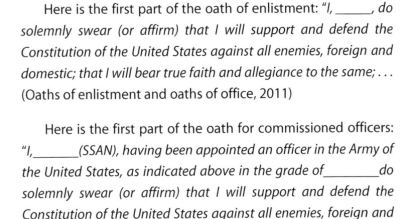

Here is the first part of the oath of enlistment: *"I, _____, do solemnly swear (or affirm) that I will support and defend the Constitution of the United States against all enemies, foreign and domestic; that I will bear true faith and allegiance to the same; . . .* (Oaths of enlistment and oaths of office, 2011)

Here is the first part of the oath for commissioned officers: *"I, _____(SSAN), having been appointed an officer in the Army of the United States, as indicated above in the grade of_____do solemnly swear (or affirm) that I will support and defend the Constitution of the United States against all enemies, foreign and domestic, that I will bear true faith and allegiance to the same; . . .* "(Oaths of enlistment and oaths of office, 2011)

Here is the first part of the oath of office for police: *"I, _____, do solemnly swear (or affirm), that I will support the Constitution of the United States, and the Constitution and laws of the State of..."*

The theme of course is the support and defense of the Constitution of the United States of America. Every single cop and every soldier took some version of this oath.

How many military and law enforcement personnel do you think can either recite the general idea of each Article in the Constitution, or even know how to reference the document in an efficient manner?

Referring to the Constitution as THE idea, we must understand that these people are tasked with a very important job; to protect and defend the idea of the United States of

America. This is not something they are forced to do, they chose that job and task.

The question is quite simple: How in the world can anyone support and defend an idea if they do not know what that idea is? Since the idea in question is the Constitution, how in the world can anyone support and defend the Constitution if they do not know what the Constitution says?

The argument that usually follows is that these people have enough to deal with without having to memorize something like the Constitution, or very few people have the Constitution memorized, so how can we expect these people to memorize it.

The retort is even simpler than the question: because it is their job. It is not like the people of this great nation are asking for much. If you are going to swear an oath to support and defend something, know what that something is. Once again, we are talking about a document the size of a short story, a few pages long, so why should we not expect this? Is this NOT the law of the land? How can they enforce it if they do not know it?

This is usually where people start splitting hairs and talking about obeying orders and so on. These are usually just excuses to help disguise the ignorance and perhaps laziness surrounding the topic. Let me demonstrate.

The Uniform Code of Military Justice (UCMJ) 809[890].ART.90 (20), makes it clear that military personnel need to obey the *"lawful command of his superior officer,"*

891.ART.91 (2), the *"lawful order of a warrant officer"*, 892.ART.92 (1) the *"lawful general order"*, 892.ART.92 (2) *"lawful order"*. (Failure to obey order or regulation) I agree with this part of the debate and concede to it. However, there is more to debate than just this.

In these cases, military personnel have an obligation and a duty to only obey Lawful orders. In addition, they have an obligation to disobey Unlawful orders, including orders by the president that do not comply with the UCMJ. That being said, the moral and legal obligation is to the US Constitution and not to those who would issue unlawful orders, especially if those orders are in direct violation of the Constitution and the UCMJ.

The Constitution trumps all. This is evident via our documentation and our oaths of enlistment, oath of office and so on. So the question needs to be presented yet again: Exactly how can someone support or defend the Constitution of the United States when they have no idea what the Constitution says? Perhaps the biggest question is how can you place your life, liberty, trust, etc., in the hands of someone who does not know this document and does not care to learn it?

To see just how scary this question really is, I challenge you to pick a section out of the Constitution and ask random military or law enforcement personnel. Article 4 Section 4 is a good one, so is Article 1 Section 9 for that matter. Just say *"excuse me sir/ma'am, you're an* (officer/soldier) *you'll know this."* Have a pen ready as though you are going to write it down. *"What is Article 4 Section 4 of the Constitution?"*—And wait for an answer.

Chances are, you will not get a coherent response and that demonstrates the point. I doubt they even have a pocket Constitution on them to reference. So the moral of this chapter is quite simple: if you want to know why the Constitution continues to get shredded, and if you want to know why your Bill of Rights are practically a memory, it is because the people who have been tasked with protecting the Constitution against all enemies both foreign (but primarily) domestic, simply do not know the document they swore an oath to defend.

This is an excellent example as to why orders of tyranny can present themselves in uniform under the guise of being there to help. It is only furthered when we consider the type of training many in uniform receive. Ask yourself the following question: Which do you think someone in uniform could more easily recite; a list of what classifies a domestic terror threat or, the Bill of Rights?

That being said, if you are an LEO and/or military personnel and you know these documents, then I commend you and thank you deeply for everything you are doing. I hope the people can continue to count on you as future events and perhaps the inevitable begins to occur. Furthermore, I encourage you to have the strength to restrain fellow officers who are violently violating the Rights of the citizenry. You took the job because you are brave; I hope you can be brave when it counts most.

To the veterans—It should also be said that your oath does not cease to exist just because you no longer hold a position. The oath does not expire. There are many who are no longer in position who swore that same oath. Let us hope you consider your actions in regard to Constitutional defense as a "*civilian*".

As for those in uniform who abuse your power, and for that matter, abuse the people you somehow think you have authority over; understand that you are not a friend of the Constitution and will ultimately be regarded as such. Your excuses for such abuses are fundamentally invalid. Ignorance of the law is no excuse. This works both ways and the Constitution trumps all whether you want to recognize this or not.

Does this seem brash? I come from a family of military and law enforcement personnel. Heck, my grandfather was brass as an LEO. I ask nothing of you I would not ask of my own. This position is often questioned though, and perhaps I need to explain it in a little more detail from a different perspective.

A friend of mine served 4 years in the Marine Corps Infantry 1st BN 2nd Marines, (2 tours Iraq, 04' and 06') and has served in Law Enforcement since 2009. He is a great man and someone I highly regard as a protector of the Constitution. He will be the first to tell you that Law Enforcement is not an easy job. From his perspective, he states that in Law Enforcement, the job is to uphold and enforce state and federal laws, dealing with every complaint, with victims, with witnesses, and a suspects

Constitutional Rights, all while attempting to satisfy their employer, the public, the media, and everyone else.

It is understood that the job of Law Enforcement is not always easy, and complexity to the job is added when we factor in the idea that officers need to keep their head on a swivel, looking out for their own safety as well as the safety of everyone else, so everyone can go home to their families at the end of the day.

Being in the military can be rough too. Granted, roughly 91 percent of military jobs do not involve direct combat operations, it is understood that the job revolves around or relates to war in some way shape or form. Many civilians simply cannot fathom this idea. In the military, the job function essentially surrounds the idea of death: either making it or taking it. This is felt even in the non- combat roles such as journalism, business administration, food service and human resources.

Regardless, does the stress associated with such jobs excuse a lack of professional behavior or blatant violations of the oath? Does this all somehow exempt the fundamental aspects of the oath these people took? After all, it is not like the job descriptions are not thoroughly discussed prior to service. The police must obey the law while enforcing the law.—Earl Warren, US Supreme Court Justice (1891-1974)

Yes these are tough jobs. No one really disputes that. However, we have to keep in mind that people in uniform voluntarily signed up to protect the people and the

Constitution. Yes, there are those who signed up for the free education or other benefits. These people joined for the wrong reason. If citizens are somehow expected to treat people in uniform as though they were touched by the hands of angels or that they should be held in higher regard or feared just because they wear the uniform, then they should be held to the standard they expect.

The people should care little about how difficult the job is. If it is too hard, then volunteering to do it should not have been an option. There are plenty of Constitution loving Americans who would gladly do the job because they want to do what is right for their communities and their nation. The job should not be an excuse for lashing out and beating a cuffed suspect or for not upholding your duties because someone outranks you. The job should not be an excuse for pile driving someone half the size of the officer into the ground or waiting until someone with a higher rank says something about the violations of the UCMJ and/or the Constitution.

And let us examine one other aspect that many refuse to even look at. When it comes to Law Enforcement personnel who violate someone's Constitutional Rights, what recourse does that person or victim have? Court?

If you search the words "*bad cop*" on the internet, it does not take long before you see repeated demonstrations of law enforcement personnel, kicking, punching, tasing, and shooting people in unbelievably excessive ways. The irony is that there is usually another cop present who does nothing about it, and the citizen receiving the abuse literally cannot do anything about it because if they are not cuffed physically, they are cuffed legally.

If the person feels as though their Rights are being violated, they cannot (in the moment) defend themselves without receiving several additional charges against them, regardless of the initial reason for being searched, detained, or even arrested. What is the recourse? A hospital bed and a court date? What does the officer get? Administrative leave and if the community is lucky, fired? Obviously, this power imbalance is not right. When these situations occur, why do the other officers go along with it?

These situations demonstrate a violation of Rights. However, you can only push a people so far. The irony is that there are well over 21.5 million people who have sworn an oath to defend our Constitution who are not currently serving in uniform. If you are one that violates the Constitution and believe you are somehow above the law, understand that you are outnumbered. You may get your licks in now, but this time will be short lived.

The people are waking up. Remember, we are a Republic. We are in this together, and ultimately, you may find your side of the tyranny paradigm rather lonely in the coming years.

Once again, if you are police and/or military personnel and you know these documents and you do your job for the right reasons, then I commend you and thank you deeply for everything you are doing. These statements are not blanket by any means and I know you are just as frustrated by the actions of those I speak. I am confident that the people of your communities and this nation can continue to count on you as the inevitable begins to occur.

Some will be questioning why such statements have been made. It is because the Oath is vital, because it tasks certain people with protecting certain Unalienable Rights. Without such Rights, one has to ask what we have at all.

Still, there is an even bigger danger lurking in this regard. Not knowing what you stand for is bad enough, but what happens when someone has sworn the oath and blatantly disregards it? We should never exclude or forget about people such as Lt. Col. Robert Bateman, who have made public statements in support of the suppression or elimination of Constitution Rights (Bateman, 2013).

These people are the most dangerous of all. Whether silent, or vocal like Bateman, we should always (as George Washington stated) *"guard against the impostures of pretended patriotism."*

The Bill of Rights

So let us explore some of our most precious Rights here in the United States.

Amendment I—Congress shall make no law respecting an establishment of religion, or prohibiting the free exercise thereof; or abridging the freedom of speech, or of the press; or the right of the people peaceably to assemble, and to petition the Government for a redress of grievances.

Amendment II—A well-regulated Militia, being necessary to the security of a free State, the right of the people to keep and bear Arms, shall not be infringed.

Amendment III—No Soldier shall, in time of peace be quartered in any house, without the consent of the Owner, nor in time of war, but in a manner to be prescribed by law.

Amendment IV—The right of the people to be secure in their persons, houses, papers, and effects, against unreasonable searches and seizures, shall not be violated, and no Warrants shall issue, but upon probable cause, supported by Oath or affirmation, and particularly describing the place to be searched, and the persons or things to be seized.

Amendment V—No person shall be held to answer for a capital, or otherwise infamous crime, unless on a presentment or indictment of a Grand Jury, except in cases arising in the land or naval forces, or in the Militia, when in actual service in time of War or public danger; nor shall any person be subject for the same offence to be twice put in jeopardy of life or limb; nor shall be compelled in any criminal case to be a witness against himself, nor be deprived of life, liberty, or property, without due process of law; nor shall private property be taken for public use, without just compensation.

Amendment VI—In all criminal prosecutions, the accused shall enjoy the right to a speedy and public trial, by an impartial jury of the State and district wherein the crime shall have been committed, which district shall have been previously ascertained by law, and to be informed of the nature and cause of the accusation; to be confronted with the witnesses against him; to have compulsory process for obtaining witnesses in his favor, and to have the Assistance of Counsel for his defense.

Amendment VII—In Suits at common law, where the value in controversy shall exceed twenty dollars, the right of trial by jury shall be preserved, and no fact tried by a jury, shall be otherwise re-examined in any Court of the United States, than according to the rules of the common law.

Amendment VIII—Excessive bail shall not be required, nor excessive fines imposed, nor cruel and unusual punishments inflicted.

Amendment IX—The enumeration in the Constitution, of certain rights, shall not be construed to deny or disparage others retained by the people.

Amendment X—The powers not delegated to the United States by the Constitution, nor prohibited by it to the States, are reserved to the States respectively, or to the people.

(US Const.)

There is your Bill of Rights. Theoretically, these were supposed to be *"Unalienable Rights"*. Unalienable by definition means *"unable to be taken away from or given away by the possessor"*.

How can that be? These Rights are taken away, amended, altered, and transferred all the time. The fact that any of these can be taken away even temporarily should be a huge wake up sign for Americans. It is bigger than that though.

Let me demonstrate that every single Amendment is currently being assaulted by the federal government in some way shape or form. While the examples for each one are substantial, for the sake of space, only two examples will be given for each Amendment to express the point. The verbiage of the Amendment will be repeated so you are not forced to jump pages.

Amendment I—Congress shall make no law respecting an establishment of religion, or prohibiting the free exercise thereof;

Example 1: Obamacare contraception requirement
Example 2: the attempt at the Federal Marriage Amendment

or abridging the freedom of speech, or of the press;

Example 1: See Something Say Something
Example 2: Justice Department subpoenas of AP emails
BONUS: Being arrested for making jokes about the TSA

Or the right of the people peaceably to assemble, and to petition the Government for a redress of grievances.

Example 1: IRS targeting of the TeaParty
Example 2: Must pay for a permit to assemble

Amendment II—A well-regulated Militia, being necessary to the security of a free State, the right of the people to keep and bear Arms, shall not be infringed.

Example 1: Signing of the UN Small Arms Treaty
Example 2: "*Assault*" weapons ban

Amendment III—No Soldier shall, in time of peace be quartered in any house, without the consent of the Owner, nor in time of war, but in a manner to be prescribed by law.

Example 1: July 10, 2011. Henderson (Nevada) city police occupied the Mitchell family home for a "*tactical advantage*" over a neighbor.
Example 2: Boston Marital Law

Amendment IV—The right of the people to be secure in their persons, houses, papers, and effects, against unreasonable searches and seizures, shall not be violated, and no Warrants shall issue, but upon probable cause, supported by Oath or affirmation, and particularly describing the place to be searched, and the persons or things to be seized.

Example 1: Warrantless wiretapping

Example 2: IRS's use of the Electronic Communications Privacy Act of 1986.

Amendment V—No person shall be held to answer for a capital, or otherwise infamous crime, unless on a presentment or indictment of a Grand Jury, except in cases arising in the land or naval forces, or in the Militia, when in actual service in time of War or public danger; nor shall any person be subject for the same offence to be twice put in jeopardy of life or limb; nor shall be compelled in any criminal case to be a witness against himself, nor be deprived of life, liberty, or property, without due process of law; nor shall private property be taken for public use, without just compensation.

Example 1: US Supreme Court ruled a suspect's silence can be used as evidence of his guilt.
Example 2: Public Danger Exception in Boston
BONUS: Eminent Domain
BONUS: Taxes

Amendment VI—In all criminal prosecutions, the accused shall enjoy the right to a speedy and public trial, by an impartial jury of the State and district wherein the crime shall have been committed, which district shall have been previously ascertained by law, and to be informed of the nature and cause of the accusation; to be confronted with the witnesses against him; to have compulsory process for obtaining witnesses in his favor, and to have the Assistance of Counsel for his defense.

Example 1: NDAA
Example 2: Bradley Manning or Anwar al-Awlaki

Amendment VII—In Suits at common law, where the value in controversy shall exceed twenty dollars, the right of trial by jury shall be preserved, and no fact tried by a jury, shall be otherwise re-examined in any Court of the United States, than according to the rules of the common law.

Example 1: TORT *"Reform"*
Example 2: Slocum v. New York Life Insurance Company

Amendment VIII—Excessive bail shall not be required, nor excessive fines imposed, nor cruel and unusual punishments inflicted.

Example 1: Drone Strike Assassinations against Citizens
Example 2: Undefined Prison Sentences & Solitary Confinement
BONUS: ISOM v. STATE (ISOM v. STATE, 1991)

Amendment IX—The enumeration in the Constitution, of certain rights, shall not be construed to deny or disparage others retained by the people.

Example 1: The Hatch Act
Example 2: Property Ownership

Amendment X—The powers not delegated to the United States by the Constitution, nor prohibited by it to the States, are reserved to the States respectively, or to the people.

Example 1: Federal Gun Ban
Example 2: DOMA

These are just examples of course, and once again, there are plenty of examples that could be used. These are just to demonstrate that every single Amendment has come under attack in some way shape or form, and yet, we do not see anyone from any branch of government stepping into stop such infringements.

Instead, we see quite the opposite do we not? We see police enforcing horrible laws that infringe on the rights of the people, and we see military carrying out assassinations against American citizens because some guy (who did NOT have citizen approval) said to go ahead and murder a citizen without Constitutional oversight!

Who is going to stand up to protect our Constitution? Exactly how much of the Constitution has to be infringed upon before enough is enough? This is not instigating mind you, these are legitimate questions. What is the recourse for violating the law of the land? Where is the resolve to hold our elected representatives accountable? Where are the freedom loving Constitutionalists who swore to uphold and defend the Constitution against all enemies both foreign and domestic?

We are literally watching our nation crumble ad everyone is afraid of the people who work for us! It is a twisted mess, and it is going to get much worse before it ever gets better.

The protection of Rights does not solely fall upon the shoulders of those in uniform. YOU have to take ownership. The Constitution does not provide you these Rights. You were born with them. The Constitution simply listed them out as Rights the government could not license, alter, adjust, trade, or take away. By resisting unconstitutional law, you are in fact acting in a Constitutional manner.

You need to know, protect and exercise your Rights. A big part of the issue is that when someone gets offended by another exercising their Rights, the person exercising said Rights is made to feel guilty about it as though they had done something wrong.

You should not apologize for exercising your Rights. Sometimes, someone may exercise a Right and you may get offended. Sometimes, someone might get offended when you exercise a Right. So what? It is yours or their Right to do so and it is your duty to not only "*allow*" it, but to encourage it. Sure, you may disagree with what they say, but it your duty to defend their Right to say it. It should be reciprocated accordingly. This should work out great as long as everyone is not infringing upon the Rights of another.

Furthermore, you do not have a Right against offense. You will be offended from time to time. Be an adult. Be responsible for your actions.

People of religious faith, stop pushing religion on everyone. Atheists, stop stealing religion from everyone. Respect the opinions of others as well as their beliefs.

We should all be allowed to have our principles. We should not only have them but be willing to stand upon them and collectively resist policies or programs that contrast with the Constitution.

We are in fact born equal. Prosperity and happiness . . . we have to chase that and we must not stand in the way of others attempting the same.

The Power to Protect

One Right sticks out more than most when we consider possible controversy of an Amendment. This of course is Amendment II. There seems to be some confusion about the limits of this Amendment and perhaps how it applies. This chapter should help to alleviate any such "*controversy*" and explain what should be the end of the debate as a whole. This chapter will also clear up some of the stigmas attached to the controversy and demonstrate the ignorance of so many.

The Amendment states clearly that a ***well regulated Militia, being necessary to the security of a Free State, the right of the people to keep and bear Arms, shall not be infringed***. (US Const.—Amend II)

In order to address this the right way, we must establish a common understanding of the words being used. It seems only responsible to use definition in regard to this Amendment since so many seem entirely confused about the purpose, restrictions, and scope of this amendment.

To begin with, we must look at the words "*bear*" and "*infringed*". "*Bear*" is not meant to represent mammals of the family Ursidae. Instead, it means "(of a person) *carry*" (Bear, n.d.). "*Infringed*" by definition, means "*violated*". (Infringed, n.d.). So for those seeking restrictions in the 2nd Amendment, the restriction was already written in as arms that someone can carry on their person, and this shall not be violated.

We also need to pay particular attention to the phrase *"well-regulated"*. In today's terms, regulated means to control or direct according to rule. However, this is not what this meant in the 1700's. Instead, *"well-regulated"* referred to the property of something being in proper working order. Something that was well-regulated was calibrated correctly and functioning as expected.

By definition, a militia is a citizen army; a military organization formed by local citizens to serve in times of emergencies, (militia, n.d.) who are not a part of any regular armed forces to include the Army, the Air force, the Marines, the Navy, the Coast Guard or National Guard (Beard, 1909).

Additionally, and again by definition, a militia is not government sponsored. This means that arms, uniforms, training, equipment, etc., are not provided by either the state or the federal government. Instead, they are provided solely by the citizen seeking participation in the militia.

You must have citizens in order to have a militia. Citizens must have arms, equipment, etc., to participate in the militia since they are not provided by the state or the federal government. If governments do not provide such arms and equipment, pray tell who might provide these? Beginning to see the point?

The *"militia"* was not given the right to bear arms. Instead, it is *"the right of the people to keep and carry arms"* as clearly stated in the Amendment.

The Second Amendment is not entirely about firearms though. This is the part that most people get confused about. The Second Amendment enumerates the right of the people to form a citizen army to protect the Free State.

The reason it was enumerated this way was because the British did not allow the colonists the right to self-protection and raised their tyrannical armies against the colonists. As mentioned earlier, as you read through the Declaration of Independence, one can clearly see the several times the founders addressed military forces set against the colonist by their own King. Oddly enough, our government today highly frowns upon the practice of citizen armies, or carrying weapons, and appears to be placing military forces against the people.

The Amendment does not say a single thing about the caliber of people that can form such citizen armies or for what reasons. Instead, it states clearly that the citizen army is necessary to the security of a free state and reiterates the idea that the right of the people to keep and carry arms shall not be violated, because the citizenry cannot form a citizen army without such arms.

To simplify, and keeping in mind that militia members are expected to bring their own arms, it is easy to see that if the citizen army was supplied by the state or the federal government, then they would (by definition) not be a citizen army at all. Instead, they would be a local state sponsored military force such as the National Guard. Just to keep the debate honest, the National Guard falls under the Department of Defense.

The reiteration of this point is extremely necessary to understand the following point. Any army needs to have access to weapons of war in order to be even remotely effective. Therefore, in order to have a properly functioning or well-practiced militia, citizens would not only have to have the right to keep and carry arms, but they would also need the ability to acquire military grade weapons capable of being carried on their person that were effective at accomplishing their mission of securing a free state against all enemies, both foreign and domestic.

It would be pointless to form a citizen army if the people could not arm themselves as members of a legitimate citizen army. This is basic logic and it is amazing that people can interpret this any other way that than what has been demonstrated here. Simply stated, any attempt to take away, limit, or otherwise impede one's right to keep and carry arms is in direct contradiction and violation to the 2nd amendment and several other provisions of the Constitution.

The Constitution does not state that certain people were not allowed to keep or carry arms. In fact, it states quite the opposite. It says that the right to keep and carry arms shall not be violated. It does not talk about the style, size, amount, or capability of the firearm; it says what the person can carry. It does not talk about age, criminal history, or reasons for owning, it says your Right will not be violated.

Our Founding Fathers wanted this and said it was vital to the survival of freedoms and the security of our states. Only an idiot lacking both a vocabulary and a dictionary can debate this to the contrary. Granted, there are some who pull at strings of the heart stating that certain criminals should not be able to own or carry firearms, but even this retort is simple: did they not have criminals during the time of the writing of the Constitution? Do you think the founders somehow forgot to mention their intentions on the Second while addressing criminals in other areas of the Constitution? Furthermore, if the people we release from incarceration are so dangerous, then instead of stripping them of Creator given Rights, perhaps releasing them in the first place might be revisited considering there has never been a full-proof law.

Please, understand this last point. It is THIS Amendment that solidifies your power within the Republic. In order to remain free, you have to be able to counter oppressive forces, be they domestic or foreign. So let me offer you a modern translation of the Second Amendment.

Because a practiced citizen army is necessary to the security of your Republic, your right to keep and carry firearms shall not be violated.

I could inundate you with well over a hundred quotes and case precedent about the legitimacy of the points presented in this chapter. It is however, entirely unnecessary. Our founders were brilliant men. Most of them were much more educated than the average citizen today. They did not make mistakes in their verbiage. They scrutinized and thought hard about what they were doing. Their verbiage was double checked and pondered by everyone involved. Several of the people who reviewed these documents were lawyers.

It says what it says and it means what it means because our founders wanted it to be that way. To insinuate anything else is not only asinine but also a great insult. The recurrent theme throughout the documents is a great distrust of the authority which oppresses. Is it odd now that when that distrust comes up again, it is somehow a bad thing, rather than heroic or patriotic? Should this not be some kind of warning sign or red flag for the rest of us?

There are some, (usually lawyers) who try to contort the meaning of the Second Amendment. The strongest debate against what I have laid out for you here is President Jackson's declarations during the Nullification Crisis. The second is Lincoln's warning to the South in 1861. These are invalid for several reasons. To begin with, just because a President says something, does not mean it is reality. (Please Note Obama's Promises on ACA) Second, these statements were made LONG after the Constitution was already in place and agreed upon. Third, both of the Presidents listed are guilty of Unconstitutional acts and attempting to justify doing so for the sake of bigger government. This is a great segue into my final point.

The Second Amendment was not a mistake. It is an integral part of our Bill of Rights, we must reflect upon the idea *"that a bill of rights is what the people are entitled to against every*

government on earth, general or particular, and what no just
government should refuse, or rest on inference" (Jefferson, 1787).

Understanding the validity of that statement, can anyone explain how the right meant to restrict government; (a right that cannot be licensed, altered, adjusted, or taken away) is being licensed, altered, adjusted, and taken away by the very government it was meant to restrict and protect us from? The answer is simple: we have given them permission via our inaction and/or ignorance.

This may be the biggest warning you receive in your entire life. I suggest you read this chapter at least one more time for clarity.

Let me end this chapter with an interesting parallel. Texas A&M University Law Professor Mary Margaret Penrose recently called for repealing and replacing the Second Amendment during a symposium on constitutional gun rights at the University of Connecticut's School of Law.

As Hugh McQuaid reported on CTNewsJunkie, *Penrose asked the audience—a room packed full of lawyers and law school students—how many of them felt the legislative and judicial responses to gun violence have been effective. Not a single hand went up.*

"I think I'm in agreement with you and, unfortunately, drastic times require drastic measures," Penrose said. *" . . . . I think the Second Amendment is misunderstood and I think it's time today, in our drastic measures, to repeal and replace that Second Amendment."*

Rather than applying the amendment to all states, Penrose recommended striking the provision to enable individual states greater discretion in determining their own gun policies.

Penrose said she advocates redrafting the entire U.S. Constitution when she teaches constitutional law courses. She said American life has changed drastically since the 18th Century when the constitution was adopted.

"Why do we keep such an allegiance to a constitution that was driven by 18th Century concerns? How many of you recognize that the main concern of the 18th Century was a standing army? That's what motivated the Second Amendment: fear of a standing army," she said (McQuaid, 2013).

My retort is simple. In the next chapter you will clearly see that we face the same concerns today as our Founders faced in the 18th century. Professor Penrose must have a contorted view of reality or she is entirely too sheltered. Regardless, you are about to see how such ideas and words are beyond dangerous when we consider the truth in contrast to lawyers like Penrose who make, interpret, and judge the laws.

In the spirit of historical record, let us look to the words of Androcles, (son of Theodorus) when it comes to tyranny. "*Many of you might claim that desperate times call for desperate measures, and indeed you are right. I beg you, however, not to fall for the strange charm that this despotic rule may have. We are indeed in desperate times, times in which our city is weaker in both body and spirit than it has ever been. And it is for this reason that we must not allow tyranny to irreparably corrupt our core beliefs*" (Androcles, 400+B.C.). I could not agree more.

Part 2 – The Problems We Face Today

Is There Really A Police State?

Do you feel as though law enforcement enforces laws which are unconstitutional? Do law enforcement officers seem a little bit overzealous in regard to exercising their perceived authority? What do you feel when you see a cop behind you? Chances are that the majority of you will answer these questions in a negative light. This even includes those who currently serve in uniform, as I have heard the complaints and the jokes. Perhaps the best question to ask is *"Do we really live in a police state"*?

In order to effectively answer this question, one must first understand what a police state really is. Simply seeing an abundance of law enforcement or equipment does not necessary mean you are living in a police state and neither do all the references to *"1984"*. To have an actual police state, there are a couple of criteria that must be present first.

A police state is a totalitarian state controlled by a political police force that secretly supervises the citizens' activities. A more detailed way to say this would be that it is an order of police who are put in place that are not recognized by the Constitution, who enforce a system of government that is centralized and dictatorial and requires complete subservience to the state while also secretly supervises the citizens' activities.

This illustrates our current state of affairs. It is kind of creepy how spot on this really is. One could begin to see why so many would suggest that such a state even exists when we acknowledge that the NSA is listening in on conversations, or that we are being watched without consent via traffic, highway, and stoplight cameras. Never mind that these actions violate the Constitution, why are people not angry in general? Regardless, to give the benefit of the doubt, let us explore this in a little more detail.

The Agencies to Consider:

Discoverpolicing.org states that there are many different types of law enforcement agencies, from small town police departments to large federal agencies. To date, there are roughly 65 federal agencies and 27 offices of inspector general that employ full-time personnel authorized to make arrests and carry firearms. Federal officers' duties include police response and patrol, criminal investigation and enforcement, inspections, security and protection, court operations, and corrections (Types of Law Enforcement Agencies, 2013).

State and Local Law Enforcement Agencies make up the next tier of law enforcement with more than 17,000 state and local law enforcement agencies in the United States, ranging in size from one officer to more than 30,000. These are comprised of several different jurisdictional areas.

Local Police—municipal, county, tribal, and regional police that derive authority from the local governing body that created it. This is usually a corporate law situation and not a Constitutional law situation. The primary purpose is to uphold the laws of the jurisdiction, enforce UCC law, provide patrol, and investigate local crimes.

State Police / Highway Patrol—State police often perform police duties to include highway patrol and statewide investigations. State police usually assist local police with investigations and emergencies that extend beyond the resources and jurisdictional boundaries of the local agency and the power is derived out of permission from the state itself.

Special Jurisdiction Police—These include parks, schools and universities, hospitals, housing authorities, and government buildings. Their authority is derived from the local governing body that created it as well.

Sheriffs and Deputies—Generally sheriff's offices are granted authority by the State Constitution to enforce state law at the local county level. The Sheriff is publicly elected and Deputies commonly run the local jail, serve warrants and court summons, and respond to calls for service in areas outside local police jurisdictions.

Immediately we have a problem. Why does only one agency actually derive their authority by the Constitution? Why are the majority of the agencies not led by publically elected officials?

The Growing Beast:

In the face of new developments such as the NSA spying program and persistent problems such as the drone program, many have begun to speculate whether the United States is a police state, as though it were not entirely obvious. One could argue that the NSA and the drone programs are the least of our worries. Yes, they are a problem, but the bigger issue hits a little closer to home.

Each year, Congress introduces thousands of bills. Multiple thousands to be exact. These bills, represent nothing more than multiple thousands attempts of the government trying to increase their influence over you. Now, the number of bills introduced that actually make it into law is usually between 100 and 400. As a matter of fact, between 1947 and 2012, Congress has passed over 20,500 laws (Davis, 2012).

That is over 20,500 new ways to have some kind of control over your lives. Keep in mind that this does NOT include Executive orders, state or municipal laws or even the regulations within the laws that are already passed. For instance, the Affordable Care Act (aka Obamacare) has over 20,000 pages of regulations "*associated*" with the new law. You can imagine how many different regulations were slammed into the over 20,500 laws passed. If you ever needed a reason for Congress to slow down, this would be it, keeping in mind of course that each law is essentially a new restriction. Land of the free?

This results in the idea of enforcement. The first question you should ask yourself is exactly how any enforcement agency would be able to memorize or be an expert in even a fraction of this amount?

The laws around us continue to grow like weeds, but so does the size of law enforcement. It has to, and when we consider the interconnectedness of law enforcement in our nation today, we must understand that the DHS carries a ridiculous amount of weight in regard to being able to infringe upon your Constitutional Rights. This is due in great part to their influence over local law enforcement, arguably your last line of defense against Constitutional infringements.

The DHS even has "*The Office for State and Local Law Enforcement*" whose purpose is to "*keep the law enforcement community up-to-date on department-wide activities and initiatives such as "*If You See Something, Say Something*", the Blue Campaign, Nationwide Suspicious Activity Reporting (SAR) Initiative (NSI), and the Department's efforts in Countering Violent Extremism*" (DHS, 2013).

The scary part about this office is that they work with the Federal Emergency Management Agency (FEMA) to ensure that law enforcement and terrorism-focused grants to state, local, tribal, and territorial law enforcement agencies are appropriately focused on terrorism prevention activities (DHS, 2013). This is scary because of who they now classify as potential terrorists; you! So you essentially pay for your own targeting and scrutiny via taxation.

It is true that the relationship between local and federal is primarily informational. Information sharing between federal, state, and local agencies is a key element of the US government's homeland security strategy. For federal officials, the post-9/11 threat environment requires a *"trusted partnership"* among federal, state, and local agencies to *"make information sharing integrated, interconnected, effective and as automatic as possible in order to ensure our national security"* (Manager, 2006). To support this vision, the Department of Homeland Security (DHS) and Department of Justice (DOJ) administer more than a dozen homeland security- related information-sharing systems (GAO, 2007).

This *"vision"* is what might be of concern. The federal government, through programs established within the Pentagon and various agencies such as the Department of Homeland Security, are either donating, funding or otherwise providing a sizeable portion of military-grade gear to local police who are then employing it for use more frequently to carry out routine police duties.

This may not sound all that bad in of itself, but if one were to really consider the consequences of this simple idea, it would be hard to imagine a more dangerous scenario for the American people.

There are many who like to argue whether or not this build-up is a violation of the Posse Comitatus Act. We could go down that road, and one could also throw in the idea of National Guard participating in police actions on American soil is also in violation of this act considering they too fall under the Department of Defense now. The question at this point is really *"does it matter?"* Few civilians know what Posse Comitatus even is, and the fact is that few military or law enforcement know what it says either, so why bother?

We bother because the motivation for the law is clear. Military personnel are trained and equipped to wage war against an enemy. Police are trained to maintain order and keep the peace among their neighbors. Yet, Posse Comitatus has continually been disregarded by the Federal Government and today we have a police force trained and equipped to wage war against their enemies. We are getting it from all angles.

"On March 10 2009, after a report of an apparent mass murder in Samson, Ala., 22 military police soldiers from Fort Rucker, Ala., along with the provost marshal, were sent to the city of Samson," according to Harvey Perritt, spokesman for the US Army Training and Doctrine Command (TRADOC) at Fort Monroe, Va., as told to CNSNews.com.

It was sure nice of them to help out by breaking the law! The Army supposedly investigated exactly how and why active duty troops (not even National Guard) from Fort Rucker, came to be placed on the streets of Samson, Ala, especially seeing that neither the Governor, nor the President said it was okay to do so. After the fact, the police chief said he asked for help, but would it not have been a good idea to get permission or get some sort of check and balance in place before allowing regular military forces to get involved? The use of the regular troops is by all stretch of the imagination a violation of federal law in this case.

Naysayers will surely retort with the idea that the local PD only had a 5 man department, or that the help was needed because of the stated mission of traffic control and crime scene preservation. This is irrelevant because you cannot treat laws as a mathematical equation. If it was necessary to get more authorities on the scene, then 1) Why not the National Guard? 2) How about with Governor Approval? 3) Why not with neighboring Police Departments? 4) Or the State Troopers? 5) The County Sheriff? 6) Or better yet, any of the multiple agencies that could have responded without shredding Posse Comitatus once again? The point is simple: US Soldiers are not supposed to perform police actions in the United States.

Let us be perfectly clear: wrongful use of federal troops inside US borders is a violation of several federal laws, but primarily the Posse Comitatus Act of 1878, Title 18, Section 1385 of the US Code. I consider this action along with many other violations, as a calculated measure to test the resolve the people of the United States and to find out exactly how the people would react to such a blatant disregard for liberty. Of course, many people have been responding to these continual breaches of federal law and the authorities are responding in kind. Perhaps that is why the domestic police force is now becoming militarized.

On March 11, 2013, Ralph Benko wrote an article in Forbes magazine that illustrated what all Americans should be aware of. He pointed out how the Department of Homeland Security had attempted to purchase 1.6 billion rounds (enough to sustain a hot war for 20+ years), and *had taken delivery of 2,717* recently retrofitted 'Mine Resistant Protected' MaxxPro MRAP vehicles for service on the streets of the United States (Benko, 2013).

Citing a General Service Administration (GSA) request for proposal (RFP), Steve McGough of RadioViceOnline.com reported that the DHS had asked for some 7,000 *"select-fire"* 5.56x45mm NATO firearms because they are *"suitable for personal defense use in close quarters."* The term select-fire means the weapon can be both semi-automatic and automatic (McGough, 2013). Ironically enough, even though these firearms are *"suitable for personal defense in close quarters"*, the federal government is trying desperately to ban this type of firearm from use by American citizens.

Tanks, automatic rifles, and enough ammo for a long war? To make this clear, these are weapons of war being used for police action on American soil, keeping in mind of course that the Department of Homeland Security does not deploy overseas or wage war. Why the domestic buildup of war machines?

Recall Professor Penrose's statements from the previous chapter. Can you begin to see how naïve and unbelievably wrong and dangerous they were? She stated that the main concern of the 18th Century was a standing army, and alluded to the idea that 2nd Amendment might be outdated because of this fact.

What do you call a large body of people who are permanently organized, trained and equipped for land warfare that are maintained in times of both peace and war?

The previous defines a "*Standing Army*". Whatever name they go by is quite irrelevant. Call them the DHS or the National Clown Brigade but the result is the same. You must beware of ALL those seeking to pervert the foundation and the meaning. Times are not as different as some may lead you to believe. This includes professors of law.

As you can see, the beast is growing, but why?

What is the Threat?

The biggest question asked by most that are paying attention to this build-up is "*Why? Who is the threat?*" The short answer to that question is "*you*". So why the buildup if it is just you? This is a great question but undoubtedly, if you were to ask your regular local law enforcement official, they would either deny such a buildup or would be entirely ignorant of the buildup altogether.

In the defense of those officers, the general population has to remember that the majority of these officers were taught in public schools, may or may not have touched on Constitutional law during their studies, and are currently being trained and taught what the federal government would like them to know. Of course, what the federal government would like them to know is that anyone who might question and resist their immense power grabs are potential domestic terror threats.

This is convenient for the federal government of course because certain things like the Patriot Act and the National Defense Authorization Act spell out fairly big issues when it comes to those who oppose the *"vision"* of the federal government, but who are these supposed threats exactly?

In 2009, there were several lists distributed among law enforcement agencies, detailing out what a potential domestic terror threat might look like. These reports included the MIAC Report, the Virginia Terrorism Threat Assessment and the DHS Terrorism Threat Assessment. These were scary and have since been updated and refined due to mass cry out.

The scary part of that whole mess was that they even went as far as to say that veterans of the military were among terrorist risks to the US (Hudson & Lake, 2009). If you think about it for a minute, you will be forced to recognize that this also includes many current and former law enforcement as well. This is ironic because their reports are essentially suggesting that current military and law enforcement be on the lookout for their brothers and sisters in arms. Perhaps we are supposed to consider this an exception to the rule.

In July of 2012, a study out of the University of Maryland, (funded in part by the Department of Homeland Security) titled *"Hot Spots of Terrorism and Other Crimes in the United States, 1970-2008,"* stated that extremists include *"groups that believe that one's personal and/or national 'way of life' is under attack and is either already lost or that the threat is imminent"*, *"believe in the need to be prepared"* by taking part in *"paramilitary preparations and training or survivalism"*, or groups that are *"fiercely nationalistic"* and *"suspicious of centralized federal authority"* (Maryland, 2013).

In other words, if you think your rights are being infringed upon (as already clearly demonstrated), you are a part of or support militias or consider yourself to be a *"prepper"*, or simply love your country and/or freedoms and oppose a big government capable of taking that away, you are a potential domestic terror threat.

This study goes on of course, but the point you need to come away with is that they are targeting Americans who have a legitimate concern and are in line with Constitutional values. Of course, this study was conducted by the National Consortium for the Study of Terrorism and Responses to Terrorism (START) at the university which was reported to have received over $12 million from DHS and is listed as one of DHS's *"Centers for Excellence"* on the agency's website. No bias here I am sure.

This indoctrination of our law enforcement is not just on the national scale though. In October of 2013, I personally attended the FBI Chemical Industry Outreach Workshop. This was a class intended to teach law enforcement and security experts about the types of commercial explosives and improvised explosive devices that one could face. The problem was that even in a class such as this, the *"terrorist threat"* propaganda was spewed into the minds of those eager to learn. These terrorist threats according to those teaching the class included *"sovereign citizens"*, militia members, *"lone-wolves"*, and even survivalists (FBI, 2013).

Similar lists are plentiful and pretty much read the same. Numerous agencies put these lists out and many agencies train their people accordingly. Remember the rule of propaganda and indoctrination is the make a simple statement and repeat it often. Is this what we are to expect from modern law enforcement?

The Result:

The result is an interesting one but oddly points to a bigger picture. The buildup continues. Technology pointed against the people grows bigger. We see less policing per say and more military style enforcement. We literally see boots on the necks of citizens. We see shut downs of entire cities looking for one man while police point fully automatic weapons at the scared citizenry huddled inside their homes. Ultimately, we see a further erosion of the Constitution for the sake what THEY deem to be security.

Aside from the fact that law enforcement swore an oath to defend the Constitution, can they be held entirely responsible for their action against the Constitution? Actually they can and probably will be held for their actions regardless of their ignorance, at least at some point. The Nuremburg Trials illustrated that *"superior orders"*, often known as the Nuremberg defense will more than likely not hold up in a court of REAL law. Oddly enough, there is one sector of law enforcement that understands the gravity of what is going on and is proactively trying to inform you while also trying to protect you.

At the time of this entry, there are over 475 Sheriffs across this great nation who have stood up and publicly solidified their vow and oath to uphold and defend the Constitution against any entity (including the President) against Unconstitutional mandates or measures. Of course, there have been roughly 18 State Sheriffs Associations who have done the same (CSPOA, 2013). The biggest question you need to ask yourself right now is as follows:

If the ideas presented in this chapter (or this book) were wrong and everything was fine, why would so many Sheriff's across this nation be united in standing up to say anything about such possible infringements against the Constitution? If you can rationalize any other answer than a variation of "*There is a problem*", then perhaps you should read this chapter again.

It is hard to speculate why this divide has occurred among law enforcement, a few good guesses might include the idea that the Sheriff is a publicly elected official, or that a Sheriff is constitutionally recognized. Or perhaps it has something to do with the laws they are actually tasked with protecting.

If that is the case, then the next question has to revolve around the idea of what laws these others agencies actually enforce. Perhaps a better question might be if all these police in agencies other than the Sheriff's department swore an oath to defend the Constitution, why will they not stand up to say the same thing?

Perhaps it is because tyranny has already taken hold and even the enforcers have yet to recognize it. Of course, if they do recognize it, then we are in much bigger trouble than anyone can begin to fathom.

This chapter has undoubtedly stirred some emotions, especially for those who are currently serving in uniform. This is a good thing. Everyone reading this needs to understand right here and right now that the Constitution is NOT a suggestion. It is the law of the land regardless of whether you like it or not. Any law that is either followed or enforced that infringes upon the Constitution is invalid. By either following or enforcing such laws makes you an enemy of the Constitution. It is in fact that simple.

The reality? You are truly free . . . as long as you comply with what THEY want or say. The truth? Those who pass, support, or enforce unconstitutional laws . . . well that is just tyrannical.

Tyrannical Government – Really?

What are all these cries about tyrannical government? Why are others saying the government is NOT tyrannical? People seem confused. Do people even know what tyranny really is? In order to understand the depths of this topic, we really must break down the terms.

By definition, tyranny is cruel and oppressive government or rule (Merriam-Webster, Tyranny). Oppressive means very unpleasant or uncomfortable and cruel means causing or helping to cause suffering (Merriam-Webster, Oppressive). So ask yourself the question: Does the government rule in an unpleasant, uncomfortable manner? Does the government cause or help to cause suffering? It may seem counterintuitive, but the answer is not as easy as a yes or no. The reason why is due in great part to perspectives. Most would agree that the government has its moments where they do fit the definitions provided, but the retort is often that their intent is not to do so. Does it matter if the intent does not match the result?

Historical cases of tyranny in the United States are easy to come by. Of course, at this point, many who read that sentence immediately thought I missed the word "*not*". That sentence is correct. Examples are easy to come by. There is a frame issue at hand though. What one deems to be tyranny may not be classified as tyranny to another. For the sake of argument, we will focus on a general theme of the introduction of the

Democracy and the decay of the Republic. This begins right prior to 1913.

You are about to read one of the most important facts you have ever been exposed to. If you embrace and study this, it can fundamentally change your entire political position.

Since 1913, there have been approximately five constants in this great nation. 1) An increase in the size of government. 2) A reduction in personal liberty. 3) A continual devaluation of the dollar. 4) A continuation of policy from one administration to the next. 5) Both major political parties are responsible for the previously stated. Now take a few minutes to really ponder this. Can it be disputed?

The Size of Government and Continuation of Policy

This can almost go without saying but for clarity, we should address the elephant in the room. 1913 was a big year for the American people. We mark this day as the beginning of the end of our Republic for several reasons.

Yes, our government has grown since it was first created. This is not in dispute. However, there are certain times when the government grew substantially over other periods. This usually occurs when the ability to do so presents itself. The point you need to be aware of is that the federal income tax made that growth possible.

In 1913, the 16th Amendment to the Constitution made the income tax a permanent fixture in the US tax system. The

Federal Reserve was also created in 1913 and this should come as no surprise as the two are very much connected at the hip. Perhaps you can thank Woodrow Wilson and his corrupt attitude for this. Then of course, the Federal Trade Commission was created in 1914.

When the federal income tax was introduced, the highest tax bracket was 7 percent for all income above $20,000. Due in great part to the war; by 1918 the highest rate rose to 77 percent beginning at $4,000. In other words, the government was taking in a substantial amount of money. Over the next decade, federally owned corporations grew like weeds. Of course, this model did not stop and simply expanded the size and scope of the federal government.

Again, the US government grew substantially with President Franklin Roosevelt's administration and his introduction of entitlements. One of the largest spikes in government growth was between 1933 and 1945. Franklin Roosevelt's New Deal meant many more federal employees to handle the ever-increasing size and scope of social programs. When WWII came around, he used this as yet another tool to expand its power. During the twelve years that Roosevelt ruled, the total number of federal employees increased from a little over half a million in 1933 to an amazing 3.5 million in 1945 (US-History, 2013).

It did not stop there. The mission was set and the model worked. From 1960 to 1990, wars continued, programs were introduced, frivolous reasons were provided and the number of state and local government employees increased from 6.4 million to 15.2 million. An increase in the size of government, these programs continued from one president to the next, and both parties were and remain responsible.

The Parties

How does all this happen if there are two unbelievably different sides in the political spectrum? One is for small government, one is for bigger government, but one would think that a reduction in the size would have occurred at some point. This is actually a clue to help you understand that there really is not a difference between the two sides. They are on the same side . . . and that side is opposite of you, the American citizen. Consider the following:

Have you ever stopped to consider that perhaps two sides are not that different? Think about it: The wars in the Middle East have involved at least four different presidents. NAFTA/SPP/ Trans Pacific Partnership/etc., have spanned at least three presidents. We are literally witnessing the phrase "*Meet the new boss—Same as the old boss.*" These examples go on and on, but the effort here is to merely demonstrate the point.

Furthermore, when we really examine the platforms of each party, we begin to see that both parties are really a "*false-choice*" for the American people. For instance, how can a party be pro- life and pro-death penalty at the same time? How can a party campaign on reducing the size of government but increase government at the same time? Think about when it comes to abortion, drugs, the justice department, immigration, marital issues and sexual behavior? Does the government play a role?

On the other side of the aisle, that other party expects government to control everything (especially economic aspects), and believes government is the mechanism necessary for supporting public goods and regulating business. They demand public charity but seldom provide it themselves. They demand tolerance but provide none for opposing views and they can somehow deny government altogether when it comes to marital or sexual behavior.

These examples, too, go on for days. What you need to understand is that what you have been presented is a false choice. The truth of the matter is that if anyone were to ask you if it was okay to tell YOU how to live your life, you would tell them "*no*". Perhaps the problem is that people have too much time on their hands and feel it is somehow okay to meddle in the lives of their neighbors. It is hard to say, but irrelevant all the same.

The majority of the issues that each party represents are usually a morality issue that is state dictated anyway. The 10th Amendment states that the powers not delegated to the United States by the Constitution, nor prohibited by it to the states, are reserved to the states respectively, or to the people. This means that your state or your city will decide on the morality issues, not the President or even Congress. Why? It is because morality is not exactly addressed in the Constitution and not the responsibility of Congress. So why do these same issues continue to come up? It is because it splits the people up and keeps them distracted from the fact that they are being robbed, or worse.

George Washington warned us about the party system. He said it would tear us apart. Look at what it is has done. If you are the type to vote down party lines simply because you have some sort of hatred for this "*other side*", then you are probably more to blame than most. You are transferring power into the hands of those who would do the worst with it. Remember, over time power corrupts.

Devaluation of the Dollar

Why do things cost so much today? You probably remember your grandparents talking about how cheap things were when they were a child. This has a lot to do with inflation. This section is going to be relatively short because it simply is not that hard to figure out.

In economics, inflation is a general increase in prices and fall in the purchasing value of money (Merriam-Webster, Inflation). The government recognizes inflation as a real thing; economics recognize inflation as a real thing. The fact that inflation is real is not in dispute. Still, the media and other entities would have you believe that your dollar has not lost value. This illustrates that they think you are stupid.

The premise is quite simple though. If there is inflation in currency, there is a devaluation of that currency by definition.

So to debate this is a lesson in futility and more than likely an exercise of ignorance or stupidity.

To help you understand this a little more clearly we need a reference point. Let us start with 1913 as compared to today. If in 1913, you purchased an item at $20, then in 2013, that very same item would cost you roughly $472. This is a demonstration in the devaluation of your dollar. If you do the math on this, you will see that the majority of your dollar is gone. For the record, that means that the cumulative rate of inflation is roughly 2262.4% since 1913 (USIC, 2013).

How does this happen? Thank your privately owned Federal Reserve Bank for printing money without anything to back it. You need to understand that money is supposed to be a representation of a physical asset. If there is no real asset, there is no real value. Today, the only thing backing our currency is the idea that it is worth something and a little foreign oil. When you lose that idea and see it for what it is, the inevitable occurs.

A Reduction in Liberty

Are you free? Is your neighbor free? Better yet, do you think the government is protecting YOUR interests or their own?

Take a few minutes to look up things like The Bonus Army; an assembly of thousands of World War I veterans and their families, who marched on Washington, D.C., in 1932 to demand cash- payment redemption of their service certificates. Read about the reaction of the government and the names of the leaders who turned against their own brothers in arms. Read about the deaths of the veterans at the hands of the government (Schmidt & Hans, 1987).

Take a few minutes to look up Operation Northwoods; the proposal calling for the CIA to impose self-inflicted wounds orchestrated to appear as acts of terrorism in US to bolster public support for a war against Cuba. AKA: False Flag Operations (DOD, "*Justification for US Military Intervention in Cuba (TS)*", 1962).

Take a few minutes to look up the Kent State Massacre; the shooting of unarmed college students by the Ohio National Guard on Monday, May 4, 1970 (Laurent, Spring 2001).

And while the offenses could be listed page after page, some who are reading these words are already justifying the actions of the federal government as though they had justifiable reason. Shame on you.

Then, when adding in things like the Patriot Act, the National Defense Authorization Act, etc., we see that our situation is becoming even more horrendous. The Patriot Act (and the PATRIOT Sunsets Extension Act of 2011) destroyed your 4th amendment rights (among others). The government can review your personal effects such as email, internet activity, and cell phone activity without a warrant and, in many cases, without your knowledge. The National Defense Authorization Act destroyed your 5th, 6th, 7th and 8th amendment rights. Anyone can potentially be arrested and held without trial indefinitely, placed in confinement, etc.

Both the Patriot Act and the National Defense Authorization Act, in conjunction with the deliberate targeting by the NSA only further illustrates the point and the complete lack of regard the government has for its people. Obviously, the government does not trust the people. Once again, people are justifying these actions because they believe it is being done for their protection regardless of the fact that their TRUE protection (the Constitution) is being destroyed.

We will talk about this in more detail in the coming chapters, but consider the IRS and their tactics. People are committing suicide in this great nation due to the threats and actions of the Internal Revenue Service. People are downright afraid of the IRS. Why? It is because the government will be more than happy to destroy your lives if you cross them. Think about the targeting of News Reporters or the Tea Party.

This also brings into question the unbelievably high tax revenue the government continues to acquire at a time when the people need their money the most. Tax revenues for US states soared to their highest in 25 years in the second quarter of 2013 as personal income tax collections reached record amounts according to US Census data. This is not a new thing though, as demonstrated earlier in this chapter. However, what you need to understand is that with each increase in tax revenue, comes a substantial increase in the size of government and/or government regulation.

Ask yourself if the government rules in an unpleasant or uncomfortable manner? Does the government cause, or help to cause, suffering? The answer is an un-debatable and quite emphatic *"Yes!"* You learned early on in this chapter that the federal income tax made the growth of the federal government possible. So if the government is out of control and utilizes the income tax and the IRS for their tyrannical ways, it only makes sense that the elimination or drastic reduction of this tyranny lies within the same entity.

The Economic and Dollar Decline

The government and the media try to sell you on the idea that at the beginning of 2014, the national debt was just over 17 trillion. That number needs to be bumped up a little though. According to the US National Debt Clock, the TOTAL debt of the United States was actually well over 60 trillion dollars. That puts each American on the hook for much more than you could ever afford. You need to understand that regardless of whether or not the debt is 17 trillion, or 60 trillion, it has become impossible to pay it off due to the sheer size of it. This means that there will be an inevitable reaction to this fact.

In the fourth quarter of 2011 alone, 49.2 percent (estimated 151,014,000) of Americans had received benefits from one or more government programs, according to data by the Census Bureau (Census U., 2011).

Research on the Senate Budget Committee shows that from fiscal year 2009 to 2013, the US had spent about $3.7 trillion on 80 different means-tested poverty and welfare programs. To provide some perspective, this is roughly five times the amount spent on transportation, education, and NASA spending combined. (Halper, 2013) Enrollment in the Supplemental Nutrition Assistance Program has more than doubled in the past decade even during times of economic growth, according to US researchers.

A majority of Americans with 401(k)-type savings accounts are accumulating debt faster than they are setting aside money for retirement. According to recent reports, three in five workers with defined contribution accounts are "*debt savers*," meaning their increasing mortgages, credit card balances and installment loans are outpacing the amount of money they are able to save for retirement (Fletcher, 2013).

The dollar is failing. The gradual erosion of the dollar's status as the world's reserve currency has become more than evident as of late, due in great part to the inability to create a strategy to deal with the over $126 trillion of unfunded liabilities. So everyone is on the same page, the unfunded liabilities are the future and actual debts for which no current funding is available. This funding is not available because the amount is simply too high. In fact, there is not even enough gold on the planet to touch this amount. In fact, at $1600 an ounce, you would have to find almost 16 times more than the total amount of gold already on the planet to pay this off. The scary part is that this number increases substantially each day.

Economist John Williams says "*They are not going to address the long term solvency problems of the United States. That's going to trigger a massive decline in the dollar in the not-too- distant future, and that, in turn, will give us the early stages of hyperinflation in this next year. We're basically at a point where we can't kick the can down the road. This is it . . . . Going forward from here, you're going to generally see a weaker dollar, and it will get much weaker. You're going to have a dollar panic*" (Williams J., Early Stages of Hyperinflation Next Year, 2013).

What exactly is hyperinflation? Essentially, hyperinflation is extremely rapid or out of control inflation. It is a situation where the price increases are so out of control that the concept of inflation is meaningless. An example could be that during the time it took to eat a hamburger, the price of that burger doubled, tripled, or quadrupled. This is the reality of hyperinflation, and when it happens, it happens so fast that money becomes worthless, often within the course of the day.

Instantly, people want to deny the possibility of such an event. Normalcy bias has a way of keeping us from facing horrible realities such as this. Yet, in recent history alone, you can find almost forty examples of hyperinflationary events around the globe. You need to understand that the warning signs are not hard to miss, because we have seen it happen before.

The sad part is that we are doing this to ourselves and the ignorant masses have no idea about the cause and effect of the situation. One of the biggest warning signs of the death of our dollar boils down to easy money and low interest rates resulting from quantitative easing (QE). You have probably heard of this term in the last several years. The media has boasted it as a "*shot in the arm to the economy, fueling the stock market and helping the housing recovery*".

Nothing could be further from the truth. You have to understand that the Fed accomplished quantitative easing by "*printing money*" to buy Treasuries, and through the massive power of its purchases, it drove interest rates to record lows.

This is not exactly a good thing. The part that people miss here is the idea that they BOUGHT these. This means that the Fed has accumulated an unprecedented balance sheet of well over $3.5 trillion which needs to be dealt with.

It does not help one bit that the media continues to tell the public that our debt is one number when the true debt is substantially higher. No doubt the public is confused by the unbelievable mess that has been created, compounded by the unbelievable disinformation campaign the government seems to be engaged in.

This can all be very complicated for those who are not economically savvy. The point is, you do not necessarily have to be an economic wizard to understand the depths of the problems we are about to face. When we hear people like financial analyst Dr. Jim Willie say: *"What's going on with the Treasury bond market right now is systems are breaking, they broke the interest rate swaps. They are not functioning anymore. Foreigners are dumping Treasuries"* (Willie, 2013). Simple words like *"breaking"* or *"broke"* or *"dumping"* are words that I think most can understand.

Precious metals expert David Morgan illustrated the problem best when he said *"You cannot print yourself out of this mess that we are in. We have a massive debt problem, and the only solution they can come up with is 'add to the debt.' That will not fix the problem. The problem is the money will become worth less and worth less and nearly worthless at some point in time."* As

Morgan puts it, *"We are getting very close to the edge"* (Morgan, 2013).

These continual increases in the debt limit are obviously not a good thing. Yet, both the media and President Obama himself attempted to tell the people that it was a necessary evil or that it did not equate to a higher debt load. Blatant lies and the people accepted them because they want so desperately to believe that the government will save them.

It is not just here in the states though. Nations throughout the world are trying desperately to get rid of their dollar positions. Many have actually brought sound debates to the table suggesting that many of our recent wars were merely to retain the power of the dollar. The same idea would suggest that we will need future wars to continue on.

Regardless, in the interim, nations are stepping away from the dollar. In 2010, China and Russia announced that they would renounce the US dollar and use their domestic currencies in bilateral trade (Besta, 2010). In April of 2013, Australia announced that it was dumping the US dollar for the Chinese Yuan because the direct conversion would slash costs for thousands of businesses (Villarreal, 2013). Another great example was when China and Brazil agreed to trade in each other's currencies just hours ahead of the BRICS summit in South Africa, saying that the Chinese Yuan and Brazilian Real would be used for transactions, significantly lowering costs for the two nations (Roberts, 2009).

These are just a few examples of many. Notice a recurrent theme in regard to China and the idea that using the US Dollar actually costs other nations money? Think about this for a second. Imagine the devaluation of the dollar. Imagine a global reserve currency other than the dollar. Imagine a hyperinflationary event. It is beginning to happen right now, but you have to ask yourself *"Why?"* and *"What can happen as a result?"*

Our dollar is actually something called *"Fiat"* currency. A fiat currency is inconvertible paper money made legal tender by a government decree. In other words, the government says it is money. That does not mean it really is money and that does not necessarily mean it is worth anything.

Nick Jones of Agora Financial, LLC described fiat currency best: *"The history of fiat money, to put it kindly, has been one of failure. In fact, EVERY fiat currency since the Romans first began the practice in the first century has ended in devaluation and eventual collapse, of not only the currency, but of the economy that housed the fiat currency as well"* (Jones N., 2013).

These are powerful words and words I think many should hear. Today we see that the dollar has lost a great portion of its value, we hear threats of hyperinflation, and nations around the world are dumping the dollar. Why? It is simple. Because the dollar is dying.

This is usually where people begin the debate the actual value of the dollar. Many different stats and perspectives are brought into the equation. Ultimately though, we need to look at this rationally.

One needs to understand that the dollar is paper money that is NOT actually backed by any substantial asset. IE: Gold, Silver, etc. It used to be. Now it is just backed by interest which YOU are responsible for. Sure, some could argue that it is currently backed by oil (Petrodollar), and this is correct but we know this is unsustainable and actually just solidifies the point. Regardless, bankers print that paper money of out of nothing more than paper and ink and you work extremely hard to acquire it.

The irony is that you put your trust into this paper, and regardless of Constitutional provisions, it (for some reason) can evidently be taken away from you at any time for just about any reason. (Think inflation, market crash, taxes, etc.)

Can this paper buy you things? Sure it can, but not NEAR as much as it could when the Federal Reserve was not around. It could be argued that the Federal Reserve is directly responsible for the death of the dollar. Since the Federal Reserve came into existence in 1913, the dollar has lost over 95 percent of its value (Pilon, 2009). Today's dollar is worth less than a nickel compared to the pre-1913 dollar. THIS is probably why everyone in your house needs a job to merely get by.

It is getting worse (though few want to acknowledge this). On Feb 6, 2012, Forbes ran a story titled "*The Federal Reserve's Explicit Goal: Devalue The Dollar 33%*" (Kadlec, 2012). Think about that. Devalue the dollar 33% of what is left out of the

95% they have already destroyed? Still, few want to see the reality of what is about occur.

"*The Federal Reserve Open Market Committee (FOMC) has made it official: After its latest two day meeting, it announced its goal to devalue the dollar by 33% over the next 20 years. The debauch of the dollar will be even greater if the Fed exceeds its goal of a 2 percent per year increase in the price level*" (FRB, Federal Open Market Committee, 2013). And you did not have a say in it. You did not vote for it. Yet, it is happening all the same.

"*Quantitative Easing*" is not helping. In fact, it is destroying what is left. "*US equities have passed irrational valuation levels across the bulk of sectors and the market has become uncomfortably close to an unsustainable level that is ripe for a sizable and likely volatile correction. Where we are today is a direct result of the Federal Reserve's quantitative easing program instituted to date*" (Eliovits, 2013). And where we are, is in big trouble.

A few months ago, Forbes said "*When the Fed's problems become recognized by non-economists it will become public enemy #1 as both liberal and conservative politicians wake up to the fact that quantitative easing wasn't free. Talking heads will accuse the Fed of over stepping its mandate and Fed independence will be booty to be snatched from the ground like candy fallen from a smashed piñata*" (Sunshine, 2013).

The system does not look at your money as private property either (which you have a Constitutional right to have), just the actual property you purchase with it. And even that could be debated at times.

Still, people cannot figure out why they cannot get ahead. Of course, these same people think that the Federal Reserve is a government agency and think that somehow the numerous entitlement programs we have are somehow okay . . . even though the FED RES has to print even more money out of thin air to fund such programs . . . which of course just perpetuates the cycle. Their ignorance is duly noted.

For clarification, the Federal Reserve's own website states "(The Federal Reserve) *is considered an independent central bank because its monetary policy decisions do not have to be approved by the President or anyone else in the executive or legislative branches of government, it does not receive funding appropriated by the Congress, and the terms of the members of the Board of Governors span multiple presidential and congressional terms*" (FRB, Who owns the Federal Reserve?, 2013).

For more clarification and just so everyone is on the same page, the government is not gaining by this. The privately held banks are. Actually, the government itself is in a similar boat to you, although you could consider them the traitors that allowed it to happen in the first place. I read it best "*It is now mathematically impossible for the US government to pay off the US national debt. You see, the truth is that the US government now owes more dollars than actually exist. If the US government went out today and took every single penny from every single American bank, business and taxpayer, they still would not be able to pay off the national debt. And if they did that, obviously American society would stop functioning because nobody would have any money to buy or sell anything*" (Watson, 2013).

Definition of Assets: *a useful or valuable thing, person, or quality.*

Notice that the definition does not say "*money*". Of course, "*valuable*" lends to the idea that our FIAT currency is not an asset anyway. YOU are an asset though. You are an asset to them, because you are such a good worker! And for those who do not work . . . such a great tool necessary to keep money printing.

Keep in mind, I am not a financial adviser and this is not necessarily financial advice, but it seems to me that if you own assets and eliminate personal debt, you have a slim chance at getting ahead. At the very least, surviving what seems inevitable at this point.

A good friend once put it into perspective for me saying that in 1912, you could buy a suit and a gun for an ounce of gold. Today, you can still buy a suit and a gun for an ounce of gold. The same simply cannot be said for the value of the dollar. In 1912, the average house cost $5,935, the average car $690. Should we just assume that quality of the product is the reason for the increase?

The question was provided early in this chapter as to what the result of this might be. Perhaps the real question is whether or not economic collapse is a real possibility? Yes it is, and it is probably going to happen sooner rather than later. There are several reasons why. Probably the best reason is because of the idiots running the show who try to deceive the people. By doing so, we are keeping real possible solutions from coming to fruition or even being presented.

For instance, in a recent speech at the Business Roundtable headquarters in Washington, D.C., Obama said "*Now, this debt ceiling—I just want to remind people in case you haven't been keeping up—raising the debt ceiling, which has been done over a hundred times, does not increase our debt; it does not somehow promote profligacy (spending extravagantly). All it does is it says you got to pay the bills that you've already racked up, Congress. It's a basic function of making sure that the full faith and credit of the United States is preserved*" (Obama, 2013).

Yes America . . . this person was elected to be President of the United States. Scary is it not? Our current state of affairs should come as a shock to no one. First of all, imagine any household in America getting away with this logic in practice. Do the laws of economics somehow cease to exist in Washington? Second, it makes you wonder about things like sequestration and government shutdowns, not to mention the over $59.8 trillion dollar debt right? Perhaps he is right though, and while everyone can clearly see that the debt keeps rising each and every time they raise the debt ceiling, perhaps we should give him the benefit of the doubt and just keep moving on the direction we already are regardless of the mountain of ice we see off the bow.

Maybe Obama was simply splitting hairs. The truth is that raising the debt ceiling does NOT (in fact) raise the debt in of itself. Instead, it is the POLITICIANS who raise the debt when the ceiling is raised, giving them room to do so. So make up your mind America. Is Obama right or is he just being deceitful and trying to confuse the people? In the spirit of being equal, perhaps he is just an idiot and does not understand these basic ideas himself. Occam's Razor.

It is not that complicated, but Obama went on to suggest that "the average person" *mistakenly thinks that raising the debt ceiling means the US is racking up more debt*" (Obama, 2013). Once again, Mr Obama "*mistakenly*" thinks you are a moron and cannot figure this out on your own and he is splitting hairs to sell his position. He is banking on the idea that you are ignorant actually. Understand though that this is not entirely on the shoulders of Obama. This game was played with Bush, Clinton, Bush, etc. The worst thing you can do is attempt to point the finger at any one administration.

Maybe if our money was backed by something substantial rather than the governments "*word*" or a foreign nation's natural resource, we would not be in this position. As far as "*profligacy*" goes, I do not find it wise to debate nomenclature in this regard, but perhaps someone can demonstrate an area of government spending that is efficient and/or cost-effective, or perhaps even "*responsible*".

Maybe we are being too critical. Let us once again extend a benefit of the doubt. Perhaps we can all at least agree that their spending may not be "*extravagant*", but instead . . . perhaps they just lack restraint when spending money the people are on the hook for. (Anyone get that?)

Finally, we cannot talk about economics without talking about jobs. When we talk about unemployment, many are often confused about the numbers they hear. According to the Bureau of Labor Statistics, the mainstream media, and the White House estimates, the US continues to gain jobs all over the place. Oddly enough, the nation's official unemployment rate held steady between 7.2% and 7.9% throughout most of 2013 (BLS, 2013). How does that work?

In order to understand this, there are a couple things people really need to know. First, you need to know what a bad unemployment rate is, and second, you need to understand the model or scale they are pulling the numbers from.

A bad unemployment rate would be similar to what we saw during the Great Depression. During the depression, unemployment peaked at 24.9% in 1933. That is pretty rough. That simply means that roughly a quarter of the people were out of work. Thankfully, during our recession, we have not seen such numbers . . . or have we?

The Bureau of Labor Statistics (BLS) currently measures six types of unemployment, U1 through U6. Essentially, these break down like so:

U1 unemployment: Those who have been out of work for 15 weeks or more;

U2 unemployment: Those who have lost jobs or have only been able to find temporary positions;

U3 unemployment: Those without jobs that are available for work and actively seeking it. This is the official definition of unemployment—the one we read in the headlines;

U4 unemployment: U3 + *"discouraged workers,"* or those who have looked for jobs but feel they cannot find employment because of economic conditions;

U5 unemployment: U4 + *"marginally attached workers,"* or those who would like to find jobs but have not looked recently;

U6 unemployment: U5 + part-time workers who cannot find full-time jobs for economic reasons. This is the widest definition of unemployment and gives the most accurate picture of the total number of under-employed people (Filip, 2010).

If you are hearing about the U3 numbers in the headlines, and these are the numbers that are consistently about 7.5%, would that not allude to the idea that perhaps unemployment is actually much higher than what you have been told?

Of course it does. For instance, Forbes ran a report in July of 2013 that stated that the *"official"* unemployment rate doesn't count discouraged workers who have settled for part-time jobs or have given up looking altogether, and demonstrated how the *"U-6"* rate was actually 14.3%

(Diamond, 2013). However, they should have dug a little deeper.

This rabbit hole does not end at 14.3%. There is yet another set of numbers that I feel you should probably know about. This set of numbers is called the SGS Alternate Unemployment Rate. This is a seasonally-adjusted rate that reflects current unemployment reporting methodology adjusted for SGS-estimated long-term discouraged workers, who were defined out of official existence in 1994 by Bill Clinton (Williams J., Alternate Unemployment Charts, 2013). You read that correctly. Since 1994, the long-term discouraged workers, those who have been discouraged for more than one year, have been excluded from all government data because evidently, they simply do not count anymore.

That estimate is added to the BLS estimate of U-6 unemployment, which includes short-term discouraged workers. Actually, to make this a little more clear, this is how they tracked unemployment numbers during the Great Depression. So why did Bill Clinton change the way they track these numbers? Well, lower unemployment rates look good and keep everyone under the impression that everything is okay.

For months, people would hear about the hundreds of thousands of jobs lost, but the unemployment rate remained low. Few questioned why. How can this be exactly? Well, the answer is in the numbers you are not being told about. According to the way they tracked numbers back during the

Great Depression, our real unemployment rate for July 2013 was 23.3% (Corsi, 2013). That is over three times as bad as what you were told and just below the worst part of the Great Depression.

"Surely this cannot be . . ."—the people said. *"Where are the soup lines if that is true?"* Good question! During the Great Depression, they did not have entitlement programs or other social programs. People literally had to hit the streets for their help. Today, the soup lines are at their mailbox.

Now you know why food stamps, welfare, and other benefit programs are growing while the unemployment rate remains low. It is because not only are the numbers being manipulated, so are you.

Of course, people who are out in mass trying to inform people on what is going on, are often targeted by the federal government because the government would much rather this information remain in the dark. This is why there are now free speech zones, and why we hear stories of the IRS targeting certain conservative groups.

Who knows? Perhaps you will soon hear reports about the targeting of certain authors who have taken the time to try and inform the population of such issues. For my sake, let us hope not.

Is it starting to come together for you? If not, I will close with one more simple fact. I mentioned that according to the US Debt Clock, the total long-term unfunded liabilities were at

$126 trillion? That means that each US taxpayer now has a federal-debt liability of $1.1 million . . . and rising.

Something tells me you are going to need a second job!

The Tyrannical IRS

If bias is rampant at the IRS and political targeting is a fact, what do we do? Simple answer—tear down the institution!!! The Declaration of Independence states *"That whenever any Form of Government becomes destructive of these ends, it is the Right of the People to alter or to abolish it, and to institute new Government, laying its foundation on such principles and organizing its powers in such form, as to them shall seem most likely to effect their Safety and Happiness."*

The IRS is a form or part of Government, is it not? Has the IRS become destructive to the Constitution? Taxes are an enormous issue in the United States. It seems like every election is based in some part on this very issue and as we have seen recently, we are usually promised *"no new taxes"*, then smacked with record increases. We saw it with Bush, Clinton, Bush, and even Obama. It is again, the continuation of policy from one administration to the next.

The government tells us that taxes in general fund the federal, state, and local governments. This is not entirely true though. Imagine what you might do if you found out that almost all of the money you pay in personal income tax went to pay just one bill, the interest on the debt? What if you found out that the IRS is nothing more than a federal collection agency for a privately held banking institution? Maybe this is not the right time to address these topics. Perhaps it is best if we stick with the *"official"* story for now.

Regardless, the government would have you believe that it is through these taxes that the government programs are paid. Programs usually not worth the effort to utilize and often abused. The debate is usually all about roads, bridges, welfare, social security, military, and of course the interest on our bloated debt. Not all taxes are bad though, that is to say if they are handled correctly and placed for the right reasons.

The dark side of taxes is that they are literally a gateway into big government as demonstrated earlier, so they need to be watched and scrutinized at all times. The more money the government has, the more money it can spend on new government programs. The more government programs there are the more power the government wields. The more power the government wields, the less power the people have. The less power the people have, the fewer freedoms the people will retain. The fewer freedoms the people retain, the more tyranny has an opportunity to increase. The more tyranny there is in government, the closer you get to dictatorship. It is easy to see the progression. The point is that it all starts with the all mighty dollar and what exactly that dollar is being given up or traded for.

Remember, if the government is asking for money, or, in today's world, just taking it; we do have the right to reject such a tax. After all, this is still our government. We are still in control; we just have to be united in what we are saying instead of fighting amongst ourselves. When we fight amongst ourselves the only option is for government to step in and make the decision for us. This is yet another reason why they keep you divided.

The only reason we have high taxes is because we have allowed it to happen. People continue to ask for services from the Federal Government and the Federal Government continues to provide them. They do so by exchange. They increase your taxes to pay for it.

Thomas Jefferson: "*A departure from principle becomes a precedent for a second; that second for a third; and so on.*" What he is saying, is that if you give up an inch, expect a mile to be taken. In other words, stick to the principles we know to be true and do not stray. Stay the course no matter how hard it will get.

Yes, we have to pay taxes. We need a strong military according to our Founding Fathers and we should abide by that. We need roads and we need other public works and programs, but not to the extent that we have allowed. The list of taxes is we are faced with is simply out of control.

Let us begin with the big one; Income tax. What started out as voluntary tax to help the war effort eventually grew into one of the most controversial and non-contested laws in the history of the United States. In 1913, the 16th Amendment to the Constitution made the income tax an everlasting fixture in the US tax system. The amendment gave Congress legal power to tax income and resulted in a revenue law that taxed incomes of both individuals and corporations.

However not even 20 years earlier, the US Supreme Court decided that the income tax was unconstitutional because it was not apportioned among the states in compliance with the Constitution. The question then becomes; *"Can a law declared unconstitutional in 1895 be constitutional in 1913 and beyond?"* Talk to some former IRS special agents and find out what they say about it.

How could it be unconstitutional? The government cannot take from the people without just compensation. Some might point out that the infrastructure is our just compensation. The EPA (at the time of this writing) grades our infrastructure at a *"D"*. The government also records record revenue. Something is not adding up here.

Now, it should be clarified; you do have to pay your state income tax. However, the Federal system is a sham, for a number of reasons, but primarily because it has become a tool that instills fear in the public which is against the Constitution. Now, if we correct this aspect of the situation, we might have something to talk about.

As was mentioned earlier, many people consider the money they earned to be private property. You earned it and you use it to purchase property and personal goods, does it not in turn make money your personal and private property once you have possession under legal terms? That being said, would the Sixteenth Amendment be in direct violation of the Fifth?

This argument arises because of how the last line of the Fifth Amendment reads: "*nor shall private property be taken for public use, without just compensation*." With that being said, the income tax is taken from you, and with the IRS having the right to enforce tax laws through seizure of property and income as well as through prosecution, all for a "*Federal Bank*" which is NOT even Federal to begin with. One could argue that this too is in violation of the Fifth Amendment.

Where is the compensation for taking our money for public use? Other people may receive assistance from the programs funded by taxes such as those on welfare. The problem here is that they do not pay taxes in the first place so what are they getting the compensation for? Is it assumed that the roads are the compensation, which is primarily handled by the state anyway? No, that does not add up. Perhaps it is for the military presence in over 130 nations which goes against the principles of the Founding Fathers? Surely that is not the debate.

Many people have done a great deal of research on this controversial issue. Some people believe that the sixteenth amendment was deceitfully and illegally proclaimed to be ratified in 1913. They say that extensive legal research from both state and national archives documented irrefutably that the amendment did not receive approval by the required number of states and that the Courts have refused to hear this issue. They also say that they cannot find the laws that state that you HAVE to pay it.

That seems too complicated for the Three Rule Method. Simply ask yourself how a law declared unconstitutional in 1895 can be constitutional in 1913 and beyond? Or, read the 16th Amendment and ask if that even sounds Constitutional to you. *"The Congress shall have power to lay and collect taxes on incomes, from whatever source derived, without apportionment among the several States, and without regard to any census or enumeration."*

Furthermore, it would make it pretty hard to make any citizen file a federal income tax return without surrendering their 5th amendment right not to bear witness against themselves, simply because you can be criminally prosecuted for your return or lack thereof. In other words, if you make a mistake or do owe a considerable amount of this *"voluntary tax"*, will the IRS not attempt to seize your property? Is this part not in violation of the 4th Amendment?

Income tax takes upward of 35 percent or more on generated income. This number looks to be going up considerably in the near future. This is just the money you earn. When you begin to add in every other single tax you pay, you begin to see the level of taxation we are really under is crushing. Some estimates seem to hint at anywhere from 50 to 80 percent of an American's income can be taken in taxes by the time it is all added together. We are literally being nickel and dimed to death.

What are some of these other taxes that most do not pay attention to? Here is just a sample of some of the different taxes you are probably paying.

Federal Income Tax, Federal Unemployment Tax, Workers Compensation Tax, Social Security Tax, Medicare Tax, State Income Tax, State Unemployment Tax, School or educational Taxes, State Sales Taxes, Local Sales Tax, Property Tax, Building Permit Tax, Well Permit Tax, Septic Permit Tax, Utility Taxes, Severance Tax, Corporate Income Tax, Accounts Receivable Tax, Privilege Tax, Inventory Tax, Food License Tax, Fuel permit tax, Inheritance Tax, Interest Expense, Capital Gains Tax, IRS Penalties, IRS Interest Charges, Liquor Tax, Luxury Taxes, Marriage License Tax, Service Charge Taxes, Telephone federal excise tax, Telephone federal universal service fee tax, Telephone federal, state and local surcharge taxes, Telephone minimum usage surcharge tax, Telephone recurring and non-recurring charges tax, Telephone state and local tax, Telephone usage charge tax, Vehicle Sales Tax, Vehicle License Registration Tax, Recreational Vehicle Tax, Trailer registration tax, Road Toll Booth Taxes, Toll Bridge Taxes, Toll Tunnel Taxes, Watercraft registration Tax, Gasoline Tax, Road Usage Taxes, Dog License Tax, Fishing License Tax, Hunting License Tax, Cigarette Tax, and there are several more not to mention the plethora of taxes on the way in relation to the National Health Care debacle.

Your tax life does not even end after you die. The nail in the proverbial coffin is the almighty *Death Tax*. This wonderful piece of legislation takes just under 50% of everything you have worked for and already paid taxes on (probably numerous times) because the government feels as though they have a right to acquire half of the estate. Why in the world would a government have the right to take this from the dead, or the potential inheritors? Exactly what entitles them to it? Did they not steal enough while this person was alive?

Looking forward, we are faced with more tax hikes. This is a result of more people asking for help from the Federal Government. One of the latest issues is that of healthcare. The price of healthcare has gone up so much over the last 30 or 40 years that it has become very hard for the average citizen to pay for those services on their own. The irony is that the nation continues to try to figure out a way to pay for it, instead of looking at even one of the reasons why the prices are getting so high.

The list is long and quite irrelevant to the point of this chapter though. Tax is the answer the government has. Social entitlement, if you will. As promised, the IRS will be the enforcement wing of the new socialized Affordable Care Act. The IRS, known for its brutal and unconstitutional tactics, will be the one making sure that the employed will be paying "*their fair share*". Expect more tyranny.

The Lois Lerner situation helped expose an ever-present and unfortunate situation within our government. That of course being the complete disregard, lack of respect, and complacency the government has towards its own people. People fear the IRS and what they can do. Since the (possibly illegal) inception of the 16th Amendment and for longer than many of us have been alive, the IRS has often been the punch line of many corruption and tyranny jokes at both ends of the political spectrum. There are many real reasons behind this.

Bias however comes in many forms and this was not a shock to many. For instance, the IRS does not really bother the poverty-stricken, and is often monetarily motivated not to pick on the rich. The middle class conservative has often been the target of choice because it is this class that more than likely operates small to medium sized businesses . . . which of course were also exposed to be targets during the Lois Lerner "*scandal*". This Lois Lerner situation merely put a spotlight on our social government and how it feels about Constitution loving Americans (and Capitalists) who do not buy into its social agendas.

The point is that this bias was allowed by our powerful government . . . who currently does not seem to fear the people in anyway shape or form, let alone respect them. In order for this bias to be eliminated (since we cannot seem to rid ourselves of tyrannical government), the people must regain the power that was unjustly transferred to the IRS.

Personally, I am a fan of HR 25 (the FairTax Act). Not because I believe it to be perfect, because I do not. Instead, because it is the only plan that has been researched and reviewed to any grand extent and demonstrates a clear way of reducing the out of control power of the government currently funded by the taxpayer.

The FairTax is the result of over $22 million dollars of scholarly research involving economists from Harvard, MIT, Stanford, University of Chicago, Boston University, and other prestigious universities (Huckabee, 2010). More than anything, it eliminates the organization that seems to think it is okay to instill fear in the minds of the citizenry and destroy the lives of those who either cannot or will not comply with its demands. Frankly speaking, it eliminates the tyranny being projected upon the American people by eliminating the organization responsible while still fulfilling the monetary needs of the nation. *"No income tax, no tax return, and thus no more IRS. The national sales tax would be administered through the states, which are already tooled to collect a sales tax"* (Wong, 2006).

The FairTax plan is a comprehensive proposal that replaces all federal income and payroll based taxes with an integrated approach including a progressive national retail sales tax, a prebate to ensure no American pays federal taxes on spending up to the poverty level, dollar-for-dollar federal revenue replacement, and, through companion legislation, the repeal of the 16th Amendment. This nonpartisan legislation (HR 25/S 1025) abolishes all federal personal and corporate income taxes, gift, estate, capital gains, alternative minimum, Social Security, Medicare, and self-employment taxes and replaces them with one simple, visible, federal retail sales tax— administered primarily by existing state sales tax authorities. The IRS is disbanded and defunded. The FairTax taxes us only on what we choose to spend on new goods or services, not on what we earn. The FairTax is a fair, efficient, transparent, and intelligent solution to the frustration and inequity of our current tax system.

Eliminating federal power and giving that power back to the people of the states . . . where it (Constitutionally speaking) rightfully belongs. Have doubts? Do some research on it, you may just surprise yourself.

The Social Experiment

You go to the city pound, where you see one dog after another in their tiny little cages. They appear sad, shaking, and perhaps even hungry. You do not really question the conditions of the pound; you merely want to rescue them all. After all, you love animals.

You pick a dog out and you open the gate, the dog rushes to your arms. You provide this dog with smiles and love; you take it home and feed it. This dog remains timid for the first couple weeks until it becomes utterly loyal to you.

What just happened? Well, the dog loves you because it thinks you were the one who freed him. Then you reward it for appreciative behavior with both love and food. Ultimately though, that dog is not free at all. The dog is dependent on you, and you have merely just replaced a smaller colder cage with a much nicer cage.

The dog is essentially your slave. Sure, you may indeed take good care of it and you may even love it. However, if the dog steps out of line, you will keep that dog submitted to your will. That dog is dependent on you for shelter, food, healthcare, direction, information, etc.

Over time, the dog appreciates what you give it but it also comes to expect it. Dependence and Classical Conditioning are the key components to this example here. The idea of Classical

Conditioning is brought up to demonstrate that the false reality of the dog had become hardwired over time.

During the 1890s Russian physiologist Ivan Pavlov was looking at salivation in dogs in response to being fed, when he noticed that his dogs would begin to salivate whenever he entered the room, even when he was not bringing them food. Pavlov experimented with this idea and found that hardwired reactions can in fact be learned.

What do you call training or adapting something to live in a human environment to be of use to humans? Over time, some animals become gentler and submit to human instruction—what is called domestication. In this process, an entire animal species evolves to become naturally accustomed to living among and interacting with humans.

This happens through a process of feeding, housing, and sometimes beating down a wild animal. Once an animal submits, you breed it with another animal who has also submitted, find the subordinate offspring and continue to breed them down to the desired result. Now ask yourself, what happens to the dogs that refuse their cages and refuse their treatment? You guessed it, they are put down.

This is where we shift the conversation to the idea that I am not talking about dogs. I am talking about people. People who have been shoved in their cages and forced to accept it for what they are told it is. These ideas are hardwired into them and they defend their masters unconditionally because they rely solely on their masters giving's. Understand that what I am about to cover is going to make some of you extremely angry.

Sure, we could use the analogy of *"feeding the bears"*, or any other host of analogies but that still will not let a great portion of the population truly understand what the point refers to.

Let us use association while we cover some basic facts. Southern Democrats insisted on protecting slavery in all the territories. After the Civil War, most white Southerners opposed Radical Reconstruction and the Republican Party's support of black civil and political rights. The Democratic Party identified itself as the *"white man's party"* and demonized the Republican Party as being *"Negro dominated*," even though whites were in control (PBS, 2002).

Most blacks in America voted Republican after the Civil War and through the early part of the 20th century. Blacks could not even attend the Democratic conventions in any official capacity until 1924 (Blacks and the Democratic Party, 2008). Many people forget that Dr. Martin Luther King Jr's *"I Have a Dream"* speech was actually an attempt to push Kennedy (a Democrat) to move the needle on civil rights. So how in the world could a majority of an entire race within the boundaries of a nation turn their backs on the fundamental principles they held so dear just years prior? How could leaders like Jesse Jackson and Al Sharpton lead their people in the opposite direction of where Dr. King wanted everyone to go? Power? Money?

So think about it and ask yourself: if Dr. King was really on to something, how is this great nation not filled with highly educated black conservatives? That is the answer though. Today, it seems that ONLY the intellectual and highly educated black people are conservative (not necessarily Republican). This is not a coincidence.

What happened? Well, many black people fell in love with Democrats because they thought Democrats were the ones who "*saved the day*", forgetting of course that it has always been Conservatives who championed equality and encouraged self-reliance and independence. The Democrats sold the idea that self-reliance and independence was a bad thing. Then Democrats rewarded the black people for their appreciative behavior with money, shelter, and food (and many other social programs). Ultimately though, these blacks are not free at all. More to the point, anyone who accepted these programs were no longer free. Instead, they have become dependent on these social programs and their chains have merely been replaced with a small cage. Expand on this idea for a second and realize that I am not only addressing the black population. This means that this nation is filled with slaves of all colors and creed.

The government-run education system has done little to address these ideas. In many ways, it has served to perpetuate the problem and reinforce the "*necessity*" of the programs. Meanwhile, few people are really free. They are dependent. The sad part is that the government aims to keep it this way because it equates to power. The more reliant someone is on the aid provided, the more submissive that person will be to the person or group providing that aid.

There are two massive swings in history that shifted the majority of blacks to the Democrat party. This is ironic really, especially when you consider the opening example of this chapter. The first was FDR's social experiment with the "*New Deal*". Essentially, this was giving money to the people via social programs. The second was when President Lyndon Johnson declared a "*war on poverty*," saying "*compassionate government*" was the road to prosperity for poor people (Poverty Programs Create Welfare Addiction, 2011). This, of course, has proven to be a completely and highly flawed idea. We know this to be fact based on numerous data and the basic logic that addiction cannot be cured by providing excessive amounts of dope to the addicted.

Now you need to understand that the previously stated is merely an example of the overall whole. Once again, it is not just blacks; those who have fallen victim are of every race, color, and creed. It is not hard to imagine why. The promises for these exchanges are usually fantastic and we often do not want to hear that some things are too good to be true when it is our government making such promises. But how many of their promises are hollow? We do not want to face the reality concerning the fact that all things must come to an end. But find me something that government has built that endures.

Is it logically equal and/or fair that over 49% of the population is partaking in and/or abusing a system that provides money and benefits for doing absolutely nothing, while the remaining population is forced to work and provide for the first half? We are seeing a continual expansion in the size of government by increasing the number of laws and regulations necessary to collar the benefit programs being instated. Meanwhile, people from all over the world are traveling here to get their hands on the free benefits. This is real. Someone actually thought this was a good idea!

Imagine a world WITHOUT entitlements or false benefits for a second. We would have a smaller government where excess money would line the pockets of those who produce because the government would not feel it necessary to rob domestic companies. Criminal immigration would no longer be an issue because people would come to America for the right reasons instead of coming for the benefits, and Americans could once again embrace immigrants accordingly. There would cease to be an entire class of entitlement abusers or even generational reliance on government assistance. People could actually afford healthcare and actually amass and retain their wealth because the government would not need to steal it from the middle class. Could it work? It has before, so where are these ideas being explored in academia?

This is not a difficult concept to grasp. Even children can comprehend this, and the idea has even been a central theme for some of the most popular kid's shows.

An example of this might be a children's show called SpongeBob SquarePants. However, this is not your average kids show. There are many complex ideas that the program actually covers. In fact, one episode called "*Can You Spare a Dime?*" deals directly with the point of this chapter. In this episode, the character called Squidward quits his job because he did not like what the boss was saying to him. The main character SpongeBob meets Squidward outside of the restaurant insisting that if Squidward ever needed anything, he can turn to him for such help.

Keeping in mind that Squidward made the decision to quit, it is not long before he is homeless and begging for money and living on the streets. SpongeBob sees this and decides to do what he believes is the noble thing and takes Squidward into his own home in order to take of him until he can look for a new job and get back on his feet. At first, Squidward is very appreciative and promises that just one or two nights is all that will be necessary to get himself back on his feet again.

Then the scene flashes forward to well beyond a week. One night, Squidward continues to call on SpongeBob for water, blankets, lights, etc., all while Spongebob was trying to sleep and all things that Squidward could have gotten up to get himself. The scene ends with SpongeBob falling down the stairs. Spongebob's pet Gary tries to tell SpongeBob that Squidward is taking advantage of him, but SpongeBob is in denial and refuses to hear such words. Many months later, Squidward had become completely dependent upon SpongeBob, turning Spongebob into his personal servant (Nickelodeon, 2002).

Is this not what has occurred in this nation today? It appears as though much of this nation has become dependent on their party or the government and has more or less turned it into their personal servant. However, this works in the government (and party's) favor because they understand that these people will continue to vote for them regardless of how much liberty they take away. They know this because they understand these people need their stuff that now only government can provide. The government sells the idea with phrases like "*global village*" or "*global ideals*", etc.

Let us face reality for a second. There will never be a global village of like-minded people until some alien race decides to attack the planet. Neighbors cannot even get along. People of similar faiths cannot even get along. People under the same flag cannot even get along. For crying out loud, people from different branches of the same organization cannot even get along. There will always be infighting, there will always be war.

People often say things like; "*Look at the children, they get along regardless of color or gender.*" That is true, kids do not see color or gender until they understand differences. When people talk about the children being born without prejudice, they are also talking about someone who literally thinks the world disappears when you put their hands over their eyes. So, do us all a favor and come back to reality for the rest of this discussion.

Socialism and communism cannot work for a couple basic reasons; there will always be a leader; nowhere in nature do we find utopian equality; and even these lovely children that are so peaceful, will fight over the dumbest reasons (like blowing on them, or pointing at them, and having a better lunch). It is similar to the idea that murder has been illegal since the beginning of civilization, and we have yet to figure out how to stop it or even slow it down. Heck, even our government continues to engage in the practice while hypocritically saying that citizens cannot engage in it. The point is that these ideas cannot and do not work, which means that the programs that emulate them also cannot and do not work. It is the human factor at play.

What is the point of these Social Programs? It is about power. Not just any power though, it is about acquiring YOUR power. You trade your power for their programs. Self-reliance is a gift, not a burden. Fundamental skills are a gift, not a burden. These are gifts of power that so many are squandering away.

"The New Deal is plainly an attempt to achieve a working socialism and avert a social collapse in America; it is extraordinarily parallel to the successive 'policies' and 'Plans' of the Russian experiment. Americans shirk the word 'socialism', but what else can one call it?" - H.G. Wells The New World Order 1939

Understand that you might be under their control. It is classical conditioning at its finest. *"Our job is to give people not what they want, but what WE decide they ought to have."* Richard Salent, former president, CBS News

It is so simple, even the children can figure this out. The problem is that the adults and the public education system are mentally beating the truths out of them. The only way to break free is to explore ideas that the government is telling you to avoid. Ideas like the ones you are reading in this book. Ideas like the ones Martin Luther King Jr talked about. Ideas like the ones Thomas Jefferson talked about.

True, there are always exceptions to any rule. People get sick or disabled, but how often are these programs abused? What did people do prior to these entitlements? Should such programs be so easy to receive? If such aid was difficult to acquire, at some point, would someone try to find an easier way to acquire their aid?

Is it fair? Let us pretend that you worked hard and saved up to buy a new flat screen television. You take your hard earned money to the store and you purchase the TV. You get it home, unwrap it, and set it up. You sit back in your chair, turn it on and browse the channels. As you browse, you stumble across a news report that shows that the government is giving out the same television you just bought to those who have no money. Are you happy about this? Sure, everyone wants equally, but not everyone works equally.

In reference to a joke, we find true clarity. Imagine taking your children trick or treating on Halloween, the kids put in the effort to dress up their best, they walked up and down the streets, strutting their stuff and trying to be scary for those participating. Finally, you come to a door with a sign above that reads *"Knock at your own risk"*. The kids knock on the door, a man come out grabs the bag of candy and immediately takes half of the candy. You restrain yourself long enough to ask why in the world he would do such a thing. His response: *"I'm taking this candy to give to those can't be out trick or treating tonight"*.

People often try to debate the merits of programs such as unemployment. This is invalid considering that programs like this are essentially insurance programs and they are not able to be used indefinitely. That being said, if true social programs such as social security, welfare, etc., were similar in the idea that they ran out, there would be a substantial reduction in resistance to such programs.

Social programs are NOT the answer. Socialism is a poison. In fact, there are two definitions I would like to share with you regarding socialism. I want you to really understand these because it is important to know what perhaps you, your friends, or even maybe some of your family may subscribe to.

Socialism: any of various economic and political theories advocating collective or governmental ownership and administration of the means of production and distribution of goods (socialism, n.d.).

Socialism: a transitional social state between the overthrow of capitalism and the realization of communism (socialism, n.d.).

Communism: a totalitarian system of government in which a single authoritarian party controls the things that are used to make and transport products (such as land, oil, factories, ships, etc.) and there is no privately owned property (communism, n.d.).

Today, it appears the goal is a global communist state. Is that too farfetched?

To clarify for my socially oriented friends: I am not saying that all programs that help those in need are bad. I am simply saying that revisiting, reforming, and flat out overhauling such programs, is beyond needed at this point. This perpetual state of reliance has to stop!

The Sinister Plan

I have alluded to the idea, and I am sure you have probably picked up on the idea that perhaps the government and the parties involved have some kind of sinister plan. That perhaps they are attempting to control the masses for some bigger agenda, be it for their own power, wealth, etc. Again, you are probably not going to like what you read in this chapter, but it is important for you to at least have a vague understanding of what you are up against.

"*Ultimately, our objective is to welcome the Soviet Union back into the world order. Perhaps the world order of the future will truly be a family of nations.*" President George Bush Texas A&M University 1989

It is not a stretch to say that power is crucial if you want to control. That seems to be a rather basic concept. However, YOU need to understand that in order for your power to be seized, you have to be willing to give it up. Similar to the dog example provided in the previous chapter, this can sometimes be beaten out of you, but it can also be starved out of you, "*guilted*" out of you, or just stolen because you simply did not know what you had.

"*The depression was the calculated 'shearing' of the public by the World Money powers, triggered by the planned sudden shortage of supply of call money in the New York money market . . . . The One World Government leaders and their ever close bankers have now acquired full control of the money and credit machinery of the US via the creation of the privately owned Federal Reserve Bank."* Curtis Dall, FDR's son-in-law as quoted in his book, My Exploited Father-in-Law

There are some who probably believe that a global government or a global currency is a great idea. That perhaps FINALLY, the statist wars could stop, and we could finally get along and be happy as a species. It is true that the idea of such a world seems appealing. On the other hand, I see no such evidence in the entirety of the planet and/or natural world that suggests that such a world could ever exist.

Dogs fight. Kids fight. Plants fight. Bacteria fights. There appears to be this continual battle in every living aspect of life. Perhaps it is for balance. In the case of viruses, we know it is for dominance. In our own country, we see numerous religions and political philosophies that fight all the time.

Can someone explain how a global government would solve this? Perhaps it is because the work would be forced. Perhaps the belief systems would be forced. Perhaps those who go against the grain would be put down.

The biggest problem with a global anything would be that someone or some group would control it, which would leave the people of such a world subservient to their demands. The power would be consolidated and it would not include even a hint of a democratic model, let alone the desired republican model. Once again, I am not speaking of the party system; I am referring to the government model.

You would be amazed at how many people have been working towards this global government though. Our own elected representatives, our education systems; even the mainstream media has been indoctrinating the masses for some time.

Walter Cronkite for example, an American broadcast journalist, best known as anchorman for the CBS Evening News for 19 years. His reign on television was at a time when there was no such thing as internet or *"alternate media sources"*. Essentially, he was the information. The scary part comes into play when consider his politics and his drive. Consider the ramifications of the following:

In 1999, he appeared at the United Nations to accept the Norman Cousins Global Governance Award from the World Federalists Association. He told those assembled, *"It seems to many of us that if we are to avoid the eventual catastrophic world conflict we must strengthen the United Nations as a first step toward a world government patterned after our own government with a legislature, executive and judiciary, and police to enforce its international laws and keep the peace. To do that, of course, we Americans will have to yield up some of our sovereignty. That would be a bitter pill. It would take a lot of courage, a lot of faith in the new order."*

Cronkite went on to say that "Pat Robertson has written in a book a few years ago that we should have a world government, but only when the Messiah arrives. He wrote, literally, any attempt to achieve world order before that time must be the work of the devil. Well, join me. I'm glad to sit here at the right hand of Satan."

His rhetoric just got worse. In an interview with the BBC, Cronkite described how this New World Order would take place. "*I wouldn't give up on the U.N. yet, I think we are realizing that we are going to have to have an international rule of law. We need not only an executive to make international law, but we need the military forces to enforce that law and the judicial system to bring the criminals to justice before they have the opportunity to build military forces that use these horrid weapons that rogue nations and movements can get hold of—germs and atomic weapons.*"

It gets worse though. "*American people are going to begin to realize they are going to have to yield some sovereignty to an international body to enforce world law, and I think that's going to come to other people as well,*" he said. "*It's a fair distance to get there, but we are not ever going to get there unless we keep trying to push ourselves onto the road.*"

This is a man that the people were forced to trust for their news and information, a man who appears to champion a military dictatorship where people are forced to give up their supreme power and authority.

Unfortunately, it is not just Cronkite who feels this way. Before the World Federalist Association, then First Lady Hillary Clinton said the following: "*Good Evening and Congratulations Walter, on receiving the World Federalists Associations Global Governance Award, for more than a generation in America, it wasn't the news until Walter Cronkite told us it was the news. Every night at six o'clock, we welcomed you into our living rooms and listened as you explained the complex events of the day, whether it was the space race or the Vietnam War, Presidential Elections or Peace Treaties, you were there . . . telling us in simple, yet riveting pros . . . what was happening. You became a trusted member of my family and the families across America. For decades you told us, the way it is . . . but tonight we honor you for fighting for the way it could be. We honor you for lending your voice to the cause of human rights around the world and for your lifelong commitment to international human rights law. From your reporting on the Nuremburg Trials, to your work with WFA Campaign to end genocide, you have stirred our conscious, and challenged all of us, to live closer to the words of the universal declaration of human rights. All humans being are born free and equal in dignity and rights. So thank you Walter."*

Aside from the fact that this is entirely creepy and that most Americans simply have no clue that people from media and government continue to talk about global government, global currencies, etc., it becomes unbelievably scary when we consider that it is not merely coming from the left and state ran media, but it also coming from the party that sells itself as the champion of Constitutional liberties.

"The world can therefore seize the opportunity to fulfill the long- held promise of a New World Order where diverse nations are drawn together in common cause to achieve the universal aspirations of mankind." George Herbert Walker Bush

Friends, I could dedicate an entire book to the quotes surrounding the desire and plans to establish a global government and global currency. However, even in the brief sampling that I have provided, you can clearly see that these plans are put in place and desired by both the Republicans and the Democrats. Remember the five constants. This is why there is a difference between a conservative and a Republican, or a Democrat vs Liberal. For clarity, you can in fact be conservative without being a Republican. You can be a liberal without being a Democrat. And you can love your Constitution being either conservative or liberal. That being said, I am not entirely sure you can truly love your Constitution being Democrat or Republican considering the false choice paradigm that comes with either. Progressives . . . I am pretty sure they are the devil.

Let me make clear the premise of this chapter. Power is crucial to those who want to control. Your power is inherent, but it can be taken away if you do not realize you have it or if you decide to trade it. The ultimate goal of those seeking the power you hold, have an absolutely moronic plan that will utterly fail because it goes against the laws of what nature intended. We know that Socialism and Communism will fail because they too go against what nature intended.

"Today, America would be outraged if U.N. troops entered Los Angeles to restore order. Tomorrow they will be grateful! This is especially true if they were told that there were an outside threat from beyond, whether real or promulgated, that threatened our very existence. It is then that all peoples of the world will plead to deliver them from this evil. The one thing every man fears is the

unknown. When presented with this scenario, individual rights will be willingly relinquished for the guarantee of their well-being granted to them by the World Government." Henry Kissinger, Bilderberger Conference, Evians, France, 1991 (Tyson, 2011).

Remember, regardless of whether or not you want to see the truth about the world around you is quite irrelevant. Reality is still reality, and the result is still the same.

Sovereignty is a good thing. Free Market Capitalism is a good thing. It is not the principles that are flawed; it is the unchecked corruption that is bad. Corruption gets bad when those in power allow such events to occur. Those in power are allowed these slides when the people have no recourse for the actions of their leaders.

Mancur Olson, Professor of Economics at the University of Maryland, College Park wrote a book called Power and Prosperity. In this book he demonstrated that communist countries are at a much greater risk for corruption than are democratic societies with a free market (Olson, 2002). It then comes as no surprise that Xi Jinping, the current paramount leader of China, pointed out that corruption is one of the main concerns surrounding the success of his party.

This may be why, as stated earlier in the book, that even Putin has warned against such systems of government. Do we not heed the warnings from those who have been there, when the evidence we collect and observe provide us the same conclusions?

In my humble opinion, it is not a new system that is needed. Instead, the answer lies in providing a level of fear for those in power who continue to allow the corruption and manipulations to occur in the first place.

Ironically enough, and still very much on topic, perhaps we should reflect on some of the most profound words ever used to debate socialism. Published in 1914, John Basil Barnhill said, *"Where the people fear the government you have tyranny. Where the government fears the people you have liberty"* (Barnhill-Tichenor Debate on Socialism, 1914).

Words so profound and so true that today these words are often attributed to Thomas Jefferson, Samuel Adams, or even Thomas Paine. There you have it yet again, another example of how the simplest answer is probably the right one.

Can the Ends Justify the Means?

This chapter needs to be presented as an analogy. Not because the concept is hard to grasp, but because the idea itself is probably a perspective that is both hard to look at, but also hard to answer. This book is not about taking the easy way out as far our thoughts and decisions go. We have to ask the tough questions that dig deep into your principles so as to better understand your true positions. Let us begin.

President Truman ordered the dropping of two atomic bombs on Japan during WW2. Though the numbers are merely estimates, he is believed to have effectively killed 90,000-166,000 people in Hiroshima and another 60,000-80,000 in Nagasaki within the first few months of the bombings alone (Army, 2008).

The bombs fell on Japan, but the deaths were not only military. The majority of these deaths were civilian men, women and children who wanted no part of the conflict. The bomb also killed at least 10 American POW's at the Chugoku Military Police Headquarters (Ove, 2008). So while this act did usher in the end of WW2, we must ask ourselves "*was it ethical*"?

Essentially what we are asking is "*do the ends justify the means*"? It is the old Machiavelli debate if you will. In other words, can or should someone unleash such horror if the outcome is a positive one? It almost sounds like the debate of the double negative.

In order to answer this, we must ask ourselves some very uncomfortable questions, in an attempt to understand the extremes to which this debate has, and essentially can ultimately go. Questions such as *"If you could cure cancer, and all you had to do was brutally murder a small child, could you do it?"* or *"if by ending the lives of 200,000 people, you could save millions more, could you do it?"*

These questions are okay I suppose, but they imply that A) the outcome is expected to be good and guaranteed, and B) that someone else will more than likely have to get their hands dirty and you will not be the one cutting the throats of each individual. The truth of the matter is that in both, the result is unknown and assuming it all as a positive is irresponsible.

Let us use Hitler as an example since most are at least somewhat familiar with this leader. Hitler believed that the Jews were responsible for both the collapse of the German economy and the Russian revolution, both of which presented a huge problem for Germany. Furthermore, Hitler viewed this as a continual and ever-increasing problem. Hence, he decided to eradicate the perceived problem from Germany. Did the ends justify the means? Many would say no . . . but then again, Germany lost. (We will leave out the idiocy of Woodrow Wilson in this debate.)

Was Truman acting in an ethical way when he decided kill civilians or his own countrymen? I'm going to say no. In a war, you have two sides of military personnel, trying to inflict as much damage as possible upon the enemy while the enemy is trying to do the same in return. Generally speaking, civilians are supposed to be left out of the equation in an effort to avoid collateral damage. This is because the mass murder of civilians is actually considered a war crime and a crime against humanity (Ditcham, 2004). The problem is that the winners rarely suffer consequences, while the losers suffer greatly. WW2 is the best example of this. Both sides killed way too many civilians, but only one side was considered heroic and avoided such charges. Hypocrisy?

For me this is simple; if one has to ask whether or not actions are ethical, or if the ends can justify the means, chances are there is probably a really good argument to the contrary. This is furthered in the idea that something as simple as lying or deception might be okay if the result is a positive one, such as lying to get a job or hiding something negative from a potential partner. Such instances are usually short lived and eventually discovered. Consequences usually follow. In turn, the outcome is usually a negative one, if at the very least, as far as peer perception goes.

In the end, it boils down to perception, perspective and/ or morality. What does this chapter mean to you? What is the bigger question at play? It is rather basic actually. Ask yourself the following questions:

Is it okay for someone to infringe on the Constitution of the United States for the sake of convenience or monetary gain?

Can the ends possibly justify the means if both the means and the ends are unconstitutional? Morally and ethically speaking, should you sit idly by when you know it is unconstitutional but the government persuades with rewards for remaining silent? Should we drop our Constitutional heritage for the sake of attempting some kind of social utopia that can never be realized?

This is where we are today. As demonstrated thus far in this book, our Constitution is under fire. Our principles are under fire. Many in this great nation have sold their freedoms for temporary monetary benefit with little regard for their fellow American, their children, or the nation in coming years.

The ends were promised, but the means actually destroyed the possibility of the promise. It is the worst ponzi scheme ever. The first generation got all the benefits, the following generations will pay greatly to correct it, or sell their souls to retain aspects of it, and the last generation gets left holding the bag. Either way, the outcome will not be good and you will have to decide which side you are on.

Can the ends justify the means? That is the wrong question. The question is will any of it be worth the ends?

Part 3 – The Problem We Face Tomorrow

The Coming Domestic Crisis

There is no doubt that this chapter will come across as "*negative*". In many ways, the people of this great nation have been taught to avoid the negative. This is not exactly the best approach however, as one can rarely fix a problem without first addressing what the problem is. In other words, if you close your eyes to the world, the world still exists.

As addressed earlier, our economic situation is out of control. This is actually one of the top reasons for concern when we consider the possibility of a domestic crisis.

"*I am not among those who fear the people. They and not the rich, are our dependence for continued freedom. and to preserve their independence, we must not let our rulers load us with perpetual debt . . . if we run into such debts as that we must be taxed in our meat and in our drink, in our necessaries & our comforts, in our labors & our amusements, for our callings and our creeds, as the people of England are, our people, like them, must come to labor 16 hours in the 24 give the earnings of 15 of these to the government for their debts and daily expenses; and the 16th being insufficient to afford us bread, we must live, as they now do, on oatmeal & potatoes.*

. . . And this is the tendency of all human governments. A departure from principle in one instance becomes a precedent for a second; that second for a third; and so on, till the bulk of the society is reduced to be mere automatons of misery, and to have

no sensibilities left but for sinning and suffering. Then begins, indeed, the bellum omnium in omnia, which some philosophers observing to be so general in this world, have mistaken it for the natural, instead of the abusive state of man. And the fore horse of this frightful team is public debt. Taxation follows that, and in its train wretchedness and oppression." (Excerpts from a letter from Thomas Jefferson to Samuel Kercheval July 12, 1816)

To summarize what Jefferson is saying here is that we must not allow our leaders to create enormous debt of any type because it is the people who are ultimately held liable. We have to make a decision between our economy and freedom or abundance and being a lowly servant. That if we run into such debt that government feels it is necessary to tax us in our goods, our property, our labor, and in our pleasure, and if we have to work for many hours of the day and pay the government a great portion of the money we earned, to the point where we can't even afford to live a decent life, and if we become this busy and this broke that we are just happy to get a job that pays us enough to get by, it is not right. Allowing one incident of this will lead to allowing yet more until all of your freedoms and all of your money is given to the government and what is left is distributed to the public. In a nut shell, massive debt and massive taxes are not good.

Consider what he is saying and then consider where we are. Have our rulers loaded us with perpetual debt? The government does feel it is necessary to tax us in our goods, our property, our labor, and in our pleasure, and we do have to work for many hours of the day and pay the government a great portion of the money we earned, to the point where we cannot even afford to live a decent life. Jefferson was correct. This is an injustice. Sure enough, we have allowed one incident to turn into another until all of our freedoms and all of our money is given to the government.

We are now hitting the stage where what is left is being distributed to the public. It almost makes you want to visit the grave of Mr. Jefferson and apologize. Regardless, the situation is impossible to ignore at this point and the repercussions are almost self-explanatory.

Everything has a process or cycle. Our situation is no different. The individual states get their power from the people. The federal government gets their power from the states. That is until the federal government gets strong enough to impose their will on the states, which are in-turn, forced to enforce the mandates being handed by the fed onto the people. Over time, the people who comprise the ranks of the federal government become numb to the idea that what they serve is a tyrannical system, and they are willing to act on behalf of such mandates in exchange for monetary or power benefit. Remember, throughout history, tyranny usually presents itself in the uniform of a government employee saying they are there to help.

We have all seen the news clips or read the articles that talk about a horrible incident that occurred to a fellow American. It is that one news story that demonstrates that an innocent man or woman was pushed around, beaten, or even killed by law enforcement over what was deemed a "*misunderstanding*" or a case of false identity. Rare? Perhaps.

We have seen the cases where someone had their entire lives ripped away by an arm of the government. It is the tragic ending of suicide with a note or manifesto stating that the government had taken everything away, be it their family or property, so this person was going to take for themselves, the only thing that was left . . . their life. Sometimes these things are taken away for what the government deems as the "*greater good*" or the betterment of the family unit. Rare? Perhaps.

Regardless of the frequency of occurrence, we justify these actions saying that the government must be looking out for us and knows what is good for us. We tell ourselves that the government MUST have had a good reason. But do they really? As we addressed earlier with the Lois Lerner situation where the IRS deliberately targeted the Tea Party, is that government looking out for their interests or is it just harassment?

When the government labels someone a domestic terror threat or an "*extremist*", surely there must be a good reason. For instance, people who adamantly love the United States (being nationalistic) or wishing to simply adhere to Constitutional values, perhaps even those who are suspicious of centralized federal authority . . . these are groups that the federal government has labeled potential domestic terror threats or extremists (LaFree, 2012). You have acquired and read this book. You are now a potential domestic terror threat. Can you see what I mean?

These two groups of people are potential domestic terror threats and extremists, and the government has labeled terrorists and extremists as enemies of the state. Considering that a "*threat*" is a person who is likely to cause damage or danger, an "*enemy*" is a person who is actively opposed or hostile to someone or something, and an "*extremist*" is a person who holds a fanatical political or religious view and is willing to resort to or advocates extreme action. That would mean that the government has labeled people who love their country and wish to abide by Constitutional law, and are willing to defend it at all costs as a threat; or simply an enemy!

This means that the government finds these Americans to be threats due to the fact that they differ in ideology. Logically speaking that would mean that the government neither loves their country nor wishes to adhere to Constitutional values and opposes those who would or do. Well, let the first couple chapters of this very book clarify this idea and then imagine what the repercussions of this reality could or will be.

Were you aware that FEMA was caught on camera calling our Founding Fathers the first terrorist organization in the United States (Jones, 2001)? Were you aware that Constitutional principles were somehow a threat to the United States Government? Were you aware that some of your children are being taught that the Boston Tea Party was an act of terrorism (HuffPost, 2013)?

The problem with tyranny is that it usually grows to a level that people simple will no longer stand for. The rise of historical monsters is inevitable. This means that the rise of turbulent times is inevitable because of the rise of dissidence from the citizenry living under such tyranny.

The founding principles of this great nation are under attack. That is almost impossible to dispute having read this far. However, it is not from some distant enemy force, but from a group of tyrants in your own backyard. Why are we so quick to justify tyranny? If we are not justifying it, why do we allow it?

Most simply do not know or understand just how tyrannical our government has become. Like the frog in the pot, everything may seem warm but the transition to boil has been gradual enough so that the effects are not seen or even felt.

This is not going to be easy to read but once again, we need to face the facts in order to understand and really appreciate the problems we face. What will follow is more of a listing of grievances that many in this great nation have brought to the public eye. For the sake of space and time, let us just cover some of the more recent example.

- IRS targeting of Tea Party or other citizens
- Lack of true representation or leadership
- The perpetual decline of the value of our money
- Increasing amount of Federal Mandates
- Revolving door between Government, Corporations, and Lobbyists
- The lies surrounding Affordable Care Act

- The ACA Healthcare being 'forced' on a dissenting citizenry
- Concealing facts involving attack on American Embassy and death of American Ambassador in Benghazi
- The Security and Prosperity Partnership
- Undue official influence on trials and juries— Zimmerman
- Ever increasing tax loads
- Ever-increasing laws and regulations
- The neglect of our veterans
- Ever-increasing Constitutional infringements—(as already addressed)
- Perpetual Inflation
- Perpetual National Debt
- Ever-increasing Debt limit
- The Patriot Act
- NDAA
- SOPA
- The protection of Monsanto
- Blatant indoctrination of our children
- Common Core
- Government Spying programs—NSA
- FEMA camps—post Katrina
- The growing redistribution of wealth
- The Arming of the DHS—the domestic military force.
- The blatant militarization of law enforcement
- Continual violations of posse comitatus
- The TSA

- Political Correctness
- Arming our supposed terrorist enemies with our money — Muslim Brotherhood, Al Qaeda, etc.
- Ever-increasing infringement on State's Rights
- The lies surrounding employment numbers
- Stealing our homes over tax "*debt*"—violation of the Constitution
- Stealing money from those who would stand to inherit.
- Giving tens of thousands of guns to Mexican Drug Cartels.—Operation Fast and Furious/Gun Runner
- Spying on EVERY-SINGLE American, by profiling their every phone call/text/online activity.
- Perpetual and unconstitutional wars—(Libya, etc.)
- Drone strikes against children.
- - Drone strikes against American citizens without Constitutional oversight.
- Targeting of news media reporters to force compliance
- Control of public information and opinion
- Repeated voter fraud
- Repeated concealment of Presidential records.
- Signing UN treaties regardless of the dissenting citizenry
- Suppression of investigators and whistleblowers
- Subversion of internal checks and balances
- Government officials who are somehow above the law

- The conversion of unalienable rights into so-called privileges
- Unconstitutional Executive Orders followed as though they trump the Constitution.
- The suppression of historical or national pride.
- The Bank Secrecy Act
- Sheriff Departments opposing Police Departments
- Continuation of policy from one administration to the next
- The Federal Reserve
- Unnecessary Eminent Domain
- Suppression of Speech
- Continual moral slide
- Ever-increasing size of the government
- Constant reduction in personal liberties
- Culture of dependency
- And so on . . .

Hopefully you are saying to yourself at this point, something along the lines of "*you forgot . . .*" I did not forget, but as mentioned before, this is just a small listing of reasons to consider just how horrible things have become. It is a little different when you see them listed out before you. The impact is much greater this way.

What you need to wrap your head around is that the founders had even fewer reasons to stand up against their tyrannical ruler. So if you consider the unbelievable level of those who are not paying attention at the moment in this nation today, and consider the economic inevitability, it would not take much of an imagination to visualize what would happen if one day the proverbial house of cards were exposed for what it is. Are you beginning to see or feel the potential for a coming crisis on the domestic front?

The fact of the matter is that you can only push a people so far. In many ways, it appears as though the people, as well as the government are beginning to figure this out. We can assume this by the very idea that the Department of Homeland Security seems to be gearing up for what some estimates have shown to be a "*hot war for twenty years*", and the banks and financial institutions are preparing for what seems to be some kind of financial meltdown. Furthermore, there is a "*prepping*" culture emerging into the mainstream by the citizenry. Is this all some major coincidence?

What if it is not a domestic crisis that everyone is preparing for? Sure, it seems logical that one could occur, but what if it were to come from outside the United States?

The Coming Global Crisis

Russia, China, Iran, North Korea, Syria, and so on. Oil, the petrodollar, terrorism, global economics, the UN. It really does not take much of an imagination to glimpse the possibility of a third global war. With the nations provided, a simple mistake and you have a World War scenario based on alliances alone, similar to that of the First World War but on a much larger scale.

It seems as though the United States is desperately trying to go to war with Iran and/or Syria. Of course, due to the strategic alliance between Iran and Syria, if you go to war with one, you go to war with the other, so which one comes first is irrelevant. These nations have quite a few powerful friends as well. Should we be concerned?

Gen. Wesley Clark, retired 4-star US Army general and Supreme Allied Commander of NATO during the Kosovo War, went on record March 5th, 2007 saying that the Secretary of Defense released a memo back in 2001 that described how the United States was going to take out seven countries in five years, starting with Iraq, and then Syria, Lebanon, Libya, Somalia, Sudan and, finishing off, Iran (Clark, 2007). You probably do not remember this being ran on your nightly news. Why not?

If you run a tally on his words, you will notice there are only two nations left on the list provided and those two are listed in the previous paragraph. So why? A term you need to become familiar with is "*Petrodollar*". A petrodollar is a United States dollar earned by a country through the sale of its petroleum (oil) to another country (Petrodollar, 2013). When we look at the nations that General Clark referred to, we see an interesting correlation . . . that of course being the petrodollar. Or better said . . . the defense of the petrodollar.

In other words, if an oil producing nation sells their oil to another nation, they use a United States dollar through that sale per agreements made in the early 1970's. This created stabilization for the dollar as well as demand. It would therefore become a threat to the United States' economy for these oil producing nations to sell their oil in currencies other than the United States Petrodollar. You might remember that the United States does not have a "*gold standard*". Perhaps instead, we should call it a "*Petro Standard*"?

Undoubtedly, there are some who would like to refute what General Clark was saying. Sure, his timeline was a little off as far as the resolution goes, but the result is the same. In November of 2000, Iraq began selling their oil in only Euros (Reuters, 2000). The next thing you know, Iraq supposedly had weapons of mass destruction and we were on our way to war. In 2003, the United States invaded and immediately switched the oil sales back to dollars (Hoyas & Morrison, 2003). So there is Iraq.

Libya—For several years leading up to 2011, Gaddafi was creating a new currency that was backed by gold and was supposed to replace the dollar for their oil sales. This was going to be called the Gold Dinar (Emmit, 2011). Of course, that never happened because the US and NATO forces destabilized the nation, Gaddafi was murdered, and the Libyan Central Bank was created. A gold dinar would have given oil-rich African and Middle Eastern countries the power to raise prices and demand payment in gold (RT, 2011). Do you think the US and its NATO allies could afford to let that happen?

Somalia— There has been a secret war going on there for quite some time now (Hosenball, 2013). In early 2013, the Obama administration expanded this secret war in violation of the terms of an international arms embargo, by stepping up assistance for federal and regional Somali intelligence agencies that are allied against the country's Islamist insurgency. The US presence there is more significant than most realize, hosting at least eight Predator drones, eight F-15E fighter jets, and nearly 2,000 US troops and military civilians at a base in neighboring Djibouti (Lynch, 2013).

Lebanon—The 2006 Lebanon War, also called the 2006 Israel- Hezbollah War. We could also look into the assassination of Rafic Hariri and the Cedar Revolution. This one has the US written all over it. However, it was not until 2012, that the information started to really surface. Reports from Lebanon said that the Qatari government has provided huge financial backup in the way of Petro Dollars for Salafi leaders and Syrian dissidents to help them recruit and train terrorists in Lebanon for the war on President Bashar al-Assad's government (Valiente, 2012). The very same government that the United

States has been attempting to oust. Why? Perhaps because there is not a central bank in Syria or because Syria might be a gateway to Iran?

Sudan—Southern Sudan became a sovereign State on July 9th 2011. However, on July 29, 2013, Mark Landler of the New York Times wrote an article describing how the Obama administration was aggressively trying to get the word out about "*a violent, murky conflict in a distant land*", but also he asked the question "*why single out this crisis*" (Landler, 2013)? That is a great question. Yet, in the very same article, we see the connection clear as day. "*The United States and other Western nations have poured billions of dollars into South Sudan, before and after the referendum, to try to turn a destitute land, with oil reserves but a long history of violence and little in the way of institutions, into a viable country*" (Landler, 2013). Note the oil.

The only nations left on the list are Iran and Syria and they are aggressively being pursued via sanctions and/or destabilization operations within the region. Regardless, be it a Central Bank, the Petrodollar or the oil itself, Americans are slowly but surely waking up to the idea the continual or perpetual war scenario has little to do with democracy or freedom. It seems it has more to do with dominance and power. Once again, you can only push someone so far before they decide to fight back. Pretending for a second that it really is all about the longevity of our freedoms, we would still have to fight for our resources.

If we consider the endless battles over resources, we must again concede to the idea of global war. The United States Department of Defense is one of the largest single consumers of energy in the world, responsible for 93% of all US government fuel consumption in 2007 (Lengyel, 2007). In fact, according to the 2005 CIA World Factbook, if it were a country, the DoD would rank 34th in the world in average daily oil use, coming in just behind Iraq and just ahead of Sweden. The reason this is important to note, is because it spells out *"motivation"*. If someone were to try and cut off this supply, or if there were some kind of *"shortage"*, there might be an issue.

The people have been told that there is not a shortage of oil, but this sure has not stopped the increase in price of oil or energy, and the repercussions concerning the economy and inflation have followed suit. This does lend credibility to the idea of the Petrodollar being the culprit as well as provide insight into an inevitable demise for our great nation.

Meanwhile, OPEC producers like Saudi Arabia have said they *"have the capacity to fill the gap"* in oil supply if dips occur (Heritage, 2013). However, this only demonstrates a continued reliance on a foreign nation to sustain our well-being, and it also implies that we will have the ability to both afford and transport the resource to the United States. Think about the many ways this could be stopped.

As an example, how many people have given any thought to the idea of an Iranian blockade of the Strait of Hormuz (which has been threatened numerous times)? What would that do the United States considering its massive hunger for oil? Would the US do what the Japanese did in 1941 and go to war over it? What if the Iranians were backed by the Russians? (Which they are)

What about during a dollar collapse or a hyperinflationary event when these other nations stop using the Petrodollar? Would that stop the desire or need for oil from a government standpoint? Of course not! So ask yourself how the government would acquire such resources with no money or physical asset to trade. War? What if Iran decided to go ahead and nuke Israel? What would the United States' response be? How would other nations like Russia respond? War?

There are many assumptions about such a war, most of which should be considered ignorant. These assumptions are that we would undoubtedly win such a war, and that such a war would never reach the mainland of the United States. These ideas are beyond naïve, and by believing such things, you are setting yourself up for disappointment.

Between Russia's Air Force and China's Navy alone, the United States would have their hands full. Think about this for a second. You have one nation responsible for literature such as "*Art of War*" and the other known for their abilities in Chess. What is the United States known for; baseball? It is safe to assume that the bigger nations around the world have a few plans up their sleeves.

My intent here is not to discredit the United States. Instead, it is to help you understand that the United States is neither invisible nor immune to invasion. While the governments of the world feud over resources and money, would this not affect the average citizen? Furthermore, we cannot win every war we start or get involved in. I understand that is rarely taught in schools these days, but that does not make it any less true.

Think about this, we almost lost in Korea (which ended in stalemate—not really a win), we lost in Vietnam, and some could argue that we lost (at least in part) during the Somali Civil War. So then let us look at Afghanistan, Iraq and Libya: we were told we won, but is that true? At the end of the day, insurgent groups have been keeping the "*strongest military might in the world*" busy for many years now and for what? Freedom? Freedom against what exactly and for who? Petrodollar Collapse?

What about invasion? Surely the United States is far enough away from any potential enemy that the only thing any enemy could hope to do would be to fire a missile at us . . . in which case, the US military would just shoot it down with our Star Wars programs or utilize the power of the USS Enterprise! Bad news, fantasy does not tend to play well with reality.

On the morning of March 9, 1916, Pancho Villa crossed the border of the United States with his horsemen, set fire to the city of Columbus, killed several soldiers, nabbed a few horses and guns, and the following day was back in Mexico to tell the tale (History.com, 1916). You probably do not find this to be a big deal.

Of course, everyone already knows about the Japanese invading the United States and attacking us at Pearl Harbor. Sure, many are quick to point out that this was not the mainland and that it does not count because they did not advance to the West Coast. Well, it does count.

June 13, 1942, four German operatives landed at Amagansett, New York, toward the eastern tip of Long Island. Or, we could discuss how three days later, another four Nazis came ashore at Ponte Vedra Beach, Florida, just south of Jacksonville. Their entire purpose was to wreak havoc on America's infrastructure (Lewis, 2011).

The argument at this point usually turns to technology and how superior the United States is and how these incidents were not full blown armies. True, but then again, according to the official story, it only took 19 people to fundamentally change our country in September of 2001 with one of the largest attacks on American soil in US History, and we have one of the most porous borders on the planet. So that debate is more or less irrelevant and the point still stands.

Let us not split hairs on this topic. Sometimes it simply does not take a standing army to attack an enemy. If the attack is on your soil, it is on your soil. Of course, perhaps the examples given really are not good enough. We need recent examples with big time players right?

Then let us wrap our minds around early 2006, when the Russian air force flew Tu-160 bombers undetected through US airspace during military exercises (RIANovosti, 2006). Or how back in 2007, a Chinese submarine was able to surprise American military leaders when a Chinese submarine popped up close to the massive super carrier USS Kitty Hawk off the coast of California (Hoft, 2010). For your information, "*Surprise*" also means undetected.

According to senior NATO officials the incident caused consternation in the US Navy. The Americans had no idea China's fast-growing submarine fleet had reached such a level of sophistication, or that it posed such a threat (Hoft, 2010).

During that same time frame, it was speculated that a mysterious contrail originating roughly 30 miles off the coast of California was actually the exhaust emanated from a missile, probably made in China. Missile experts said the plume was possibly launched from a submarine (Farah, 2010).

Essentially what occurred was that the Chinese snuck a submarine close to one of our carriers just a few miles off our coastline, then fired a missile and it surprised everyone. Theoretically, they could have nuked our West Coast and there would have been little our military could have done about it.

It was also reported in July of 2012 that two Russian Bear bombers were intercepted while flying near the west coast of the United States on the 4th of July, and that it was the second incident in the two weeks, where Russian nuclear capable bombers had entered, or come near US air space (Jackson G. P., 2012).

Let me reiterate that the point is merely to demonstrate that we are not invisible or immune from attack. We can be reached, we can be surprised. It can happen because there is no such thing as *"invincible"*. Our nation's biggest weakness is the arrogance of the American people thinking that such things could only happen in the movies and the ignorance to the reasons why any nation would be motivated to commit such an attack.

Try to remember what happened during the government shutdown in 2013. Now imagine that on a larger scale, for instance, during a dollar collapse or hyperinflation. Better yet, how about during a default on our debt? Would our military and/ or government be at its peak performance? Could they even respond? Evidently, the United States could not even keep our national parks open, and last anyone checked, parks do not really need anyone in government to be there in the first place.

When we are told that Iran's nuclear program is a threat, and we discover that Russia is actually putting that nuclear program together, what do we get? When we are told that Syria is a problem, but that Russia, Iran, and China have Syria's back, what do we get? When North Korea is running at the mouth again and we find out that China will defend them, what do we get? When we consider strategic alliances between any of them, what do we get? Many have already forgotten or were never told that World War 1 became a world war due to basic alliances between nations.

This is probably a good time to mention that I am not condoning military action against any of these nations. With the understanding of the reasons why these nations are an "*issue*" to begin with, I only see a big issue on the backend. I am also not telling you this to sell you on the idea of supporting one side or another. My intent here to point out that things are much worse than what we have been told and that you may have to face the repercussions of what your government is doing at some point. The fight may be brought to your backyard and for any number of reasons. It should be stressed that nations such as Russia and China are not only considering it, but are planning on it.

On November 1, 2013, Chinese state-run media revealed for the first time that Beijing's nuclear submarines can attack American cities as a means to counterbalance US nuclear deterrence in the Pacific. Media outlets including China Central TV, the People's Daily, the Global Times, the PLA Daily, the China Youth Daily and the Guangmin Daily ran identical, top-headlined reports about the "*awesomeness*" of the People's Liberation Army navy's strategic submarine force (Yu, 2013).

Former KGB analyst and dean of the Russian Foreign Ministry's academy for future diplomats Igor Panarin, has been predicting the fall of the United States for over a decade. He has based this on the economic and moral collapse that will trigger a civil war and the eventual breakup of the US. Maps of how the land would be divided up after such a collapse have even been created (Osborn, 2008).

Even Mikhail Degtyarev, a lawmaker in Russia, believing that the collapse of the US dollar is imminent, proposed a bill to his country's parliament on November 13, 2013, that would ban the use or possession of American currency (Bennetts, 2013). Whether it becomes law is irrelevant to the point. That is the point; the world is beginning to turn their backs on the United States.

Of course, we have not even covered Cuba or Venezuela yet, because as soon as we bring these two nations up, the arrogance of most American's kicks in and the statement that follows is "*we would kick their butts!*" Once again, perhaps (and only) if we were in a one on one fight, but if you are in that frame of mind, you are not thinking long-term or strategically.

Imagine that Venezuela and Cuba are nothing more than staging points. Now soak in the fact that both nations are allies with Russia, Iran, and China. Does that change some of your ideas? It should. The distance from Cuba to Florida is about 228 miles. The distance from Cuba and Venezuela is roughly 1300 miles. To put this distance into perspective, the distance from Iran to Israel is only about 860 miles.

Russia and the United States have had a sketchy relationship for years. Russia only "*recently*" became a "*democratic*" nation and its current leader is President Putin, a former KGB operative. KGB agents are just about the most communist outlaws to grace this planet. In light of their extreme opposition to a European shield, and their gracious help in building nuclear facilities in Iran, the line is pretty clear where they fall concerning US interests.

We could look at the promises made by the United States as well. We have promised support to nations like Japan, South Korea, and Taiwan. Taiwan and Japan are in long time disputes with China that will more than likely see physical war sooner rather than later, and South Korea is technically still at war with the North. Look at our situation with Syria. Bashar al-Assad appears to be a great friend to Vladimir Putin.

True, we could speculate the scenarios for days. Petrodollar, economic collapse, angry rivals, etc. The point here is not to provide you some play by play of what is about to occur; that would be impossible anyway. The point is merely to point out that tensions are high, and they are getting higher due to horrible policy and an ignorant citizenry that allowed the policy in the first place. There are a ridiculous amount of reasons as to why, but the point is moot when we consider where this is all heading.

If you can figure out the result, you can begin to see the pecking order of the players and perhaps how this may all pan out. More importantly, you will be able to plan accordingly as far as attempting to protect yourself. The bigger question SHOULD be whether or not the next big conflict will begin as civil or global. Note that I say "*begin as*", because based on what we can put together here, it appears as though it will be both at some point.

There will always be a nation on top, we are vulnerable as clearly demonstrated, and nothing lasts forever. We are not self-sufficient, our economy is based on a currency few really want, and we are vulnerable. There will undoubtedly be a country that will able to challenge the US. Perhaps, even fill the void if something devastating were to occur. There appears to be one nation preparing to take on the role. Oddly enough, we all should have seen it coming.

China on the Rise

Today we live in a world where international business is common place and often times extremely beneficial. On the flip side however, we are doing business and providing our much-needed money to many of our enemies because of it.

When anyone brings up the dangers of dealing with China, the rebuttal is almost always how much China needs the United States to sustain its growth and that how without the United States, China would not have the money it needed to continue to develop. That is nothing more than ego driven idea and a dangerous one at that because nothing could be further from the truth. The question is *"who really needs who?"* The last time I checked, it was the United States asking for help. Now, factor in this new push for globalization and a world currency . . . the dollar and the people of the US become pawns rather than players

China is forecast to spend roughly $1 trillion over the next decade buying up foreign assets, including about $15 billion to $20 billion a year on US investments, according to a recent Kiplinger Letter. It is speculated that they will be buying up energy, food production, financial services, manufacturing, and Real Estate.

They will be using our own tactics against us by taking our useless money and buying up real assets for their own gain. This is not only brilliant on China's part, but extremely dangerous for us. Of course, it is also highly enlightening for those who are paying attention. Who is to stop China? No one really! Most American businesses are in a position to simply take the deals they provide.

Something that people should be reminded of is that when we talk about modern day China, we are not talking about a democracy. We are talking about a military despotism. A dictatorship that is much more engrossed in power than it is trying to emulate the United States. Evidence in this is in China's tight grip over its people and its anti-American propaganda spoon-fed to its people. Not only is China growing in economic power, their military modernization efforts are growing as well.

Additionally, you can look at who China closely allies itself with and begin to see an amazing pattern of anti-American money and rhetoric. Russia, North Korea, Iran, Venezuela to name a few. As demonstrated earlier, recent news articles from around the world demonstrate the desire for China and their partners to step away from the dollar and American influence.

China is in the process of crushing the United States with lots of cheap goods that at one point were made right here in America. In exchange, they not only get our money from the purchase but they get the new-found demand from the companies who were forced to either move their operations to China to take advantage of that same inexpensive labor or simply close. As you can see, they are taking that money and buying our assets right out from underneath us.

In turn, the Chinese stock markets begin to increase and again, they obtain even more money to the tune of billions in investment capital from American investors. The whole time, smaller American companies and American jobs are shattered and the Chinese reap the profit as even more Americans become dependent on their cheaper goods. We are literally paying China to rid America of its livelihood. So from this point, we need to realize that China takes this money and does a couple things with it—it builds up its military and buys more factories.

Once again, it is a military dictatorship. The Department of Defense (DOD) recently issued the 2013 annual report to Congress on the Chinese military stating that the People's Liberation Army (PLA) is engaged in a massive, extensive modernization program, drawing upon the resources of a constantly expanding economy (now the world's second largest) to support improvements in not only the ground forces, but the PLA Navy (PLAN), the PLA Air Force (PLAAF), the Second Artillery (China's rocket forces), as well as space and cyber capabilities. The report provided details of various new ship classes, new fighters, new missiles, and improvements in Chinese space assets (Cheng, 2013).

Then it builds more factories to make more products for ignorant Americans. Then they take whatever is left and purchase US Treasury bonds to the tune of over millions a day. China is the world's largest foreign owner of US government debt (Treasury, 2013).

The future with US-China relations looks bleak. Nothing indicates a positive outcome when you really assess the facts. Simply hoping that China will need us is not enough to abandon our need for self-reliance and hemispheric stability, though this boat seems to have already sailed. We have paid the devil with the livelihoods of our own. When we fall, we will have only ourselves to blame. Look at the stimulus package delivered to everyone in early 2008. This money was borrowed from China and the Bailout package . . . it's the same thing. Now the goal was to get everyone to get out and buy products. The majority of the products were undoubtedly going to be Chinese. Who really won here? If we cannot afford to give a few hundred dollars to each American citizen without borrowing it from China, how in the world are we going to be able to afford the "*Affordable Care Act*" without some kind of outside assistance, or worse?

Perhaps that is a moot point. On October 13th, 2013, China's official news agency Xinhua said that "*The Founding Fathers of the United States of America created Congress for the sake of balance of power,*" and that "*They would turn in their graves if they saw their design being kidnapped for political brinkmanship*" (Xinhua, 2013).

Truer words have never been spoken. However, they also said that US fiscal failure warrants a de-Americanized world. The scary part is that in many ways, this is already underway.

As mentioned before, if the US falls, another nation will surely fill that void and China appears to be setting themselves up for that position. Yet more proof of their capabilities came in October of 2013, when Asian American News reported that China apparently feels as though its naval buildup has progressed enough to send surveillance ships to Hawaiian waters. The recent deployment is seen as Beijing's message to the US, and the rest of the world, that China can now contest the waters of the western Pacific and that the US Navy no longer has a free pass in the region (GoldSea, 2013).

This message was exacerbated when China's navy recently conducted a test of a new high-speed maneuvering torpedo that is set to challenge US ships and submarines in the Pacific. Other new weapons include China's recently deployed anti-ship ballistic missile, the DF-21D, which is designed to sink US aircraft carriers far from China's shores (Gertz, 2013). Still, many refuse to see such possibilities even when the Defense Department calls such technology a major threat.

I want you to consider the words of someone who has achieved the titles of both "*Mr. Commodities*" and "*Global Investing Guru*". He is the Chairman of Rogers Holdings and Beeland Interests, Inc., and was the co-founder of the Quantum Fund with George Soros and creator of the Rogers International Commodities Index (RICI).

The person I am introducing to you is a fellow by the name of Jim Rogers. Jim's words come as both a warning and as great advice, but you need to really listen and fundamentally understand what he is saying: "*If the 19th century belonged to Britain, and the 20th century to the United States. Then the 21st century will surely belong to China. My advice: Make sure your kids learn Chinese.*"—Jim Rogers—Worth Magazine

This coming from a man who believes in China's rise so much that he has literally moved to Singapore. Rogers says that "*China's long-term prospects are so strong that even a civil war, an economic collapse or political assassinations would only temporarily delay its emergence as a worldwide economic powerhouse . . .*" (Rogers, 2008).

Powerful stuff, but something tells me that if you are reading this book, this is not the first time you have heard about the "*Rise of China*". As a matter of fact, China seems to be associated with many of the topics concerning some of America's more pressing issues. For example, if one were to bring up America's National Debt, you would have to discuss China's lending practices. When we talk about currency stabilization or the International Monetary Fund, you will undoubtedly talk about China's Yuan at some point. In fact, a simple search for the term "*yuan global currency*" will give you more than enough information. When you look through your house and find the origin of the majority of the products you have purchased, you will pretty much be forced to talk about China.

Everything seems to have some kind of Chinese connection to it. When you hear about military advancements you will hear about China. When you hear about nations standing up to the United States, you will hear about China. Honestly, if anyone was not aware of China's fast and dramatic rise, they have either been blatantly lied to, or they have had their heads rooted deep in the sand. It does not take a PhD to see that China has literally become the factory of the world and that nation that many around the globe are turning to.

Now, we could delve into the many economic and political reasons why people like Jim Rogers (and many others) believe that China will rule in the 21st Century, but chances are you are probably not interested in the nuts and bolts. So, I will attempt to explain this in a brief manner.

Our dollar is collapsing because there is nothing to back it, except, perhaps oil. Our economy is collapsing because we are no longer producing local goods. Our unemployment rates are increasing because we are running out of money and because we are not hiring due to lack of American production and consumption. Our infrastructure is collapsing because we do not have the funds necessary to rebuild it. Our nationalist ideologies (love of country) are faltering because of the preceding and because someone thought it would be a good idea to feed the bears.

These are general statements and not meant to be blanketed of course. Yes, there are a few manufacturing facilities left in the United States, but not many. In fact, more than 56,000 manufacturing facilities in the United States have been permanently shut down since 2001 (Sutton, 2011). There are less Americans working in manufacturing today than there were in 1950, even though the population of the country has more than doubled since then (Snyder, 2013). These are rough statistics, but we have to talk about China when we discuss even these basic numbers.

According to a new report from the United States Chamber of Commerce, the US needs at least $8.2 trillion between 2013 and 2030 in energy, transportation, and water-related infrastructure projects. This is evidently a conservative estimate because it does not factor other necessary projects. This report suggests that we will not be able to get the money from dwindling US public funds, but instead that we will need to get the money from China (U.S.Chamber, 2013).

Back in 1985, our trade deficit with China was approximately six MILLION dollars for the entire year. In 2012, our trade deficit with China was 315 BILLION dollars (Census, 2013). That was the largest trade deficit that one nation has had with another nation in the history of the world. For clarification, that means we are simply buying billions more from China than what we are selling to them. A proverbial nail in the coffin might be that according to the

Economic Policy Institute, the United States is losing half a million jobs to China every single year.

Are you beginning to see the correlation? I hope you are beginning to see the trend here because we are on a rapid and dramatic decline and China is a big part of this. Ironically enough, our government is helping them every step of the way. I would like to put this into perspective for you.

About 32 cents for every dollar of US debt, is owned by the federal government in trust funds, for Social Security and other programs such as retirement accounts, according to the US Department of Treasury (Murse, 2013). These programs are being raided at an alarming rate so this money will more than likely not be there to cover this portion of the debt down the road. You might read this paragraph again for good measure.

The largest portion of US debt, roughly 68 cents for every dollar is owned by individual investors, corporations, state and local governments and foreign governments such as China. The largest foreign holder of US debt is China, which owns the debt in bills, notes and bonds, according to the Treasury. China's ownership of US debt is even larger than the amount owned by American households according to the Federal Reserve.

What this means is that the debt owned by China is substantially larger than the trust funds for Social Security and other programs such as retirement accounts. In other words, good luck paying that off.

The question you should be asking yourself is whether or not China is simply helping us out of the goodness of their hearts, or if they stand to gain from such a move, and if so . . . what? Think about this. When you take out a loan, you have to provide some kind of collateral. Collateral is something pledged as security for repayment of a loan, to be forfeited in the event of a default. A bank requires this because they would like to gain one way or another by fronting you the funds. Why would any other lending situation be any different?

Immediately, there are going to be those who would like to debate the idea that the US debt does not require collateral because it is backed by the *full faith of the US government*, which would be great if anyone had any faith left in the US Government, but I digress. If you are in this school of thought, then you really need to think about the following.

I have read some really ignorant statements about this topic over the last several years. Jim Luke, a Lansing Community College professor made one of these statements, and it expresses the lack of logical thought that seems to be going around these days.

Jim Luke evidently teaches "college principles of economics, along with the occasional Economic History, Comparative Econ Systems, and Econ Geography". Mr. Luke seems to think that the people of this great nation should stop worrying because there is no international court of claims where one country can foreclose on another for a bad debt. He says that what happens when a nation defaults on its debt is basically that the lenders just get really upset. They stamp their feet. They call serious meetings (Luke, 2011).

This has literally got to be one of the most ignorant statements in this history of economics, because many wars have been waged over commodities and to assume that another will not occur is naïve at best. I will not be able to provide you every single little piece of this puzzle in this chapter, but try to understand that I am merely pointing out that China will receive their money one way or the other.

Situation One—Yes, it is true that the loans taken out by the US government are backed by the full faith of the US Government. However, what many fail to realize is that this "*full faith*" is "*guaranteed*" via the property and assets of every living US Citizen as already pledged as collateral for the National Debt. We own it. We are our own government and nation. It is ours.

Taking it to the next step, we should consider something called Eminent Domain. Once again, there will be some who would argue that Executive Order 13406 ("*Protecting the Property Rights of the American People*") states that the federal government must limit its use of the taking of private property "*to situations in which the taking is for public use, with just compensation*" and "*not merely for the purpose of advancing the economic interest of private parties to be given ownership or use of the property taken*" (EO13406, 2006).

That order says "*limit*" not cease. Second, per Supreme Court ruling, private property and assets can be taken from one private owner and given to another private owner, even on the simple basis that the new owner would generate more tax revenue than the previous (Kelo V. New London, 2005). Big shocker, it happens all the time.

Bloomberg news has reported, that some Chinese officials have asked for a guarantee that *the US will support the dollar's exchange rate and make sure China's dollar-denominated assets are safe* (Cao & Chen, 2009).

Not the DOLLAR, but the dollar-dominated assets. It is not a stretch to imagine the US Government providing some kind of collateral for such a high debt load and it would be stupid for China to provide the aid without some kind of guarantee on the backend.

Maybe the idea of the government handing over large amounts of land to foreign nations or companies is too much for some to handle or even explore right now. Never mind the idea that it already occurs.

Situation Two—The United States is seeing its rapid decline as demonstrated throughout this book. So let us assume that China forgives our debt once we default or hyper-inflate and allows us some time to lick our wounds.

In this scenario, China fills the vacuum left by the Americans and becomes the world police. However, in this scenario, the United States government will have effectively lost control over a great portion of their territory because there simply would not be any money to pay the foot soldiers of the regime. Differences in ideology play out into the domestic crisis mentioned in the previous chapter.

Exactly how long would it take before a foreign nation such as China decided to come seize any number of the abundant natural resources available in the United States? After all, technically it would be theirs anyway having been guaranteed it via the *"full faith of the US Government"* which once again, is nothing more than you and your property.

The United States government and military currently walks into other nations as though they own the place, is it really a stretch to imagine another nation doing so to us once we have lost our power and influence?

Perhaps the idea of a Chinese invasion over an inability to pay a loan payment is too extreme for some to imagine. True, it may be extreme, but in many ways, this may be inevitable. Have you ever noticed how throughout history, when the balance of power has shifted between two nations, a battle always seems to occur between them?

Now I want to show you why perhaps the next several years may end up being some of the most turbulent times in recorded history.

Why We Know it is Coming

Every once in a while, you hear PhD's, philosophers, and writers talking about the "*coming war*", or an "*inevitable disaster*", or something along similar lines. The central theme of this book is no different. However, one should ask themselves exactly how these people can be so darn certain that such events are really on their way. Can they predict the future? Surely not . . . right? It would be much easier to pass off the possibility of a domestic or global crisis as nothing more than an unfortunate chain of events or circumstances. Logic, history, and common sense do not allow for such naïve positions.

Figuring out that war or economic catastrophe is on the way is actually MUCH easier than attempting to look into the future. In fact, it is as easy as looking into the past. You have probably heard at some point in your life that history repeats itself. Have you ever given any real thought to that idea? Have you ever really considered whether or not that statement was hyperbole or extremely accurate?

I would like to present the idea that it is not just hyperbole. The idea that history repeats itself is actually extremely accurate, but so many simply refuse to believe that history can really do such a thing. Perhaps it is because people see that we have things like computers and phones, and know that those things simply did not exist in the past, so they give little thought to the idea that history can in fact repeat itself.

The fact is when people say that history repeats itself; they are not referring to the technology or the actions of what you did this morning. Instead, they are referring to general ideas and events as a whole. For instance, these could include war, economic swings, periods of innovation, and so on. Most of these events are found to be extremely cyclical and sometimes even predictable.

Let us look at Rome for instance. During my undergraduate studies, I was in a class called "*Responsibility for the Future*". We examined numerous events in history and tried to learn as much as we could from each event. One such event was that of Rome's collapse. In my opinion, the most compelling piece of data that I reviewed was from researcher and senior policy analyst, Jim Nelson Black (Black, 1994), who claimed to have found 10 warning signs frequently present when a nation fell. He stated however, that only 3-4 factors were needed to contribute to the collapse of the country's government.

Those signs were as followed:

1. Increase in crime and general contempt for the law.
2. Loss of discipline and self-control in economic arena.
3. Increase in bureaucracy, regulation, and taxes.
4. Decline in both the quality and the importance of education.
5. Less attention paid to those qualities and principles which made the nation great.
6. Loss of respect for established religion.
7. Increasing materialism.

8. Increasing immorality.
9. Turning to foreign gods and worship.
10. Less value given to human life.

Upon review, and a little bit of compare and contrast, I found that Jim Nelson Black was correct. Many nations since Roman times have collapsed and just like he said, there were certain factors present. Hence, when the factors begin to present themselves, it is probably a good idea to start paying attention. This is an example of history repeating itself because certain factors show up before the collapse of a government.

Now, the scary part was that he had examined the similarities between the fall of Rome and twentieth-century United States. Looking at the list of signs, can you guess what he found? We really do not need to cover his findings though do we? It really is self-evident when you simply view it with an open mind.

Still other researchers have also found an interesting coloration between the demise of certain nations (including Rome) and one other extremely important factor; infrastructure, which of course has already been demonstrated to be "*lacking*".

But why stop there? There is so much more to the story. Have you heard of Dr. Alexander Fraser Tytler? Born in 1747, Tytler was a Scottish advocate, judge, writer and historian who served as Professor of Universal History, and Greek and Roman Antiquities, in the University of Edinburgh. Tytler is attributed with the theory of cycles concerning the rise and fall of nations. Today, that theory is known as *"Tytler Cycle"* (Tytler, 1834).

The theory is rather basic. What starts in bondage, ends in bondage. The actual steps are as follows:

- *"From bondage to spiritual faith;*
- *from spiritual faith to great courage;*
- *from courage to liberty;*
- *from liberty to abundance;*
- *from abundance to selfishness;*
- *from selfishness to apathy;*
- *from apathy to dependence;*
- *from dependency back again into bondage."*

We can clearly see reflections of our own nation inside of historical reference that allude to the idea that history can, and perhaps even does repeat itself, and that perhaps we are staring certain inevitabilities right in the face. Apathy? Dependence on government? Bondage?

Of course, many of the low information masses think of bondage as chains. However, upon enough research you will see that bondage also includes debt. So when you consider the nation's lack of interest or concern with the state of our Union, the fact that about half of the nation (at the time of this writing) receives some of kind of benefit from the federal government and that the majority of Americans are in some kind of debt, it is easy to see where we fall in this model.

To take it a bit further, let us look as some evidence that indicates we should be paying attention RIGHT NOW. For this demonstration we will focus primarily on the United States so you can clearly see the threat that is upon us.

Since before 1500, there appear to be a few cycles at play. The scary part is that these cycles tend to present themselves like clockwork. There is an Inflation Cycle, an Economic Cycle, and a War Cycle that appear as though they simply cannot be stopped. I am sure this is primarily due to the ignorance that these cycles exist, and utter arrogance or perhaps normalcy bias that does not allow us to believe that such things can exist.

Regardless, the Inflation cycle appears to be on roughly a 100 year cycle. This is a cycle of price inflation accompanied by what appears to be a general halt on the purchasing power of the currency. The last time this cycle showed its ugly little head was in 1901. Of course, we already know we are right in the middle of the next round of this cycle because the purchasing power is down substantially, and inflation is on the rise, threatening to skyrocket soon.

The next cycle is an economic cycle. This cycle includes several things but generally revolves around some kind of economic upheaval, expansion or contraction. This cycle presents itself approximately every 60 to 70 years.

The third cycle is the war cycle. Some have called this the generational cycle because it appears to occur about every 4th generation or approximately every 80 years.

The problem is that each cycle is not exactly independent of itself. In fact, these cycles appear to play into one another and perhaps even rely on one another to perpetuate. This seems to be especially true for the Economic Cycle and the War Cycle.

Now, it must be understood that the dates can be played with a bit on this. So, in all fairness to the point and to keep this simple and relevant, we will focus on the economic cycle and the war cycle and use the latest dates since the creation of the United States to illustrate the point. Furthermore, we will use the 60 to 80 year split since both models fall within that time period. If you would like to research further back and play with the dates yourself, you should be able to do so using the dates provided.

Historians contend that the Industrial Revolution really "*broke out*" between 1760 and 1780. This is the Economic cycle at play as this changed the economics of the world during that time substantially. More directly, it changed the way people made their money. On the cusp of this event was the American Revolution, which was between 1775 and 1783.

If we add 60 to 80 years to the end of that time period, we get a time-span of 1843 to 1863. An interesting thing occurred during this time, an enormous railway expansion began and railroads began to replace canals as a primary mode of transportation. This is an economic factor that once again changed how people made money. Right on cue, the Civil War started in 1861 and lasted until 1865.

So then we add 60 to 80 years to the end of 1865, we get a time-span of 1925 to 1945. Many of you are familiar with the great stock market crash that occurred on October 29, 1929. This would start what would later be known as the Great Depression which changed everything economically around the world and changed the way people would make their money. As you guessed, war came right along with it. World War II started in 1939 and lasted until 1945.

Now comes the interesting part. If we add another 60 to 80 years to 1945, you will notice we get a time-span of 2005 to 2025. Pay attention, because national and global economics are in an upheaval to say the very least, and the war drums are pounding louder than ever.

Some of you have already put the bigger picture together. That picture of course being that close scrutiny of the cycles presented in this chapter paint a much more horrible picture. Not just two cycles, but ALL of the cycles presented in this chapter appear to align between 2005 and 2025.

We can see we have the majority of the factors presented by Jim Nelson Black, we are definitely on the backend of Tytler Cycle, we are in the middle of the Inflation Cycle, we are currently witnessing the Economic Cycle and we are waiting on the War Cycle. We have seen all the reasons necessary and we have covered the most obvious players.

Using even basic observation, it is not hard to see where we are headed. The scary part is that it is not often that all of these events align in such a way at the same time. This leads me to believe that the level of effect will be substantially higher than ever presented before in recent history. Perhaps this is why we are seeing governments around the world prepare for what seems to be the inevitable.

Keep in mind that this information is not being shared to scare you. Instead, it is being shared to prepare you. Look at it this way, if you ignore this warning and the information is right, the result for you could be catastrophic. If you heed this warning and the information was wrong, you have lost nothing.

It can be scary to imagine what appears to be the inevitable. So many unknown factors and still trying to gauge if it will be over resources, some kind of attempt at global dominance (like WWII), or something else altogether. There are many ways this could go down. This is why it is so important that you have a solid understand of the threats before they arrive at your door.

Prepare now!

Part 4 – Perspectives and Considerations

Things you should consider moving forward…

Perhaps Ayn Rand Had It Right

What is a businessman? Is it merely a man who works in business or commerce? The book Atlas Shrugged presents characters such as Hank Rearden, and James and Dagny Taggart, as people who all engage in commerce, but whose intentions and motivations for doing so are very dissimilar (Rand, 1996). The villains and the heroes begin to show themselves and reflections of fiction begin to emerge in our own reality as the story unfolds. It is then we discover that the characters presented are not all businessmen. Wealth may be created by production however, there are those who are wealthy who have never produced a thing or even contributed to that production, yet feel as though they have the right to consume or acquire without legitimate trade. Atlas Shrugged clearly demonstrates the differences between those who earn versus those who take.

Characters such as James Taggard, Orren Boyle, and Wesley Mouch illustrate the unethical side of business. These are the villains who take from those who have produced, either for themselves to redistribute to their friends, or to redistribute to those with the power to vote and perpetuate or even exacerbate their power to take in the first place. The question one must ponder then becomes "*is it ethical to take something from someone and give it to another?*"

According to definition, redistribution is an economic theory, policy, or practice of lessening or reducing inequalities in income through such measures as progressive income taxation and antipoverty programs (Dictionary.com, 2013). Simplified of course, this model requires that someone merely take from those who have, and give to those who have not.

Imagine one having a desire for the money in a neighbor's safe, so they hire someone to acquire the money. The person who retrieves it receives a cut for his efforts. Labor, ingenuity, thought, and self-reliance were all demonstrated in this example; however, what has just occurred (according to most court systems) is burglary due to the blatant disregard for ethical standard, regardless of the premise of reducing the inequalities in income. It remains a fairly basic concept that has been demonstrated in the courts numerous times. Theft is defined as stealing. Stealing is to take (the property of another) without right or permission (American-Heritage, 2003). Clearly, no matter how you approach this, taking something from someone without their consent is wrong and unethical.

Atlas Shrugged demonstrates that money is not the measure of a man, but that what matters is how he acquired it. As suggested in the book, paper money is worthless unless it represents value through production (Rand, 1996). In other words, people trade their labor/ideas/skills/etc., in exchange for money. For some unknown reasons, the courts remain drastically divided on the matter, but the 5th Amendment to the United States Constitution states quite clearly that no one will be deprived of life, liberty, or property, without due process of law; nor shall private property be taken for public use, without just compensation (US Const.). If that is true, can it even be legal for a government to take money without legitimate trade? Perhaps the question then becomes "*is money even private property*"?

At your job, you trade your labor for money. Money is the medium in which you can acquire goods, or "*property*". Upon purchase, these goods are considered the private property of the individual who bought them because it is land or belongings owned by a person or group and kept for their exclusive use (Collins, 2003). Therefore, money and property must be one in the same. If they were not, then everything one purchased with money would technically be owned by the printer of that money. By extension, this negates the 5th Amendment altogether and renders it a moot point. This is obviously not the case however, because the preceding is valid.

So, as you can clearly see, by definition, basic logic, and Occam's Razor, taking money from one to give to another without consent is not only unethical but is also legally, Constitutionally, and morally wrong, regardless of who tries to say it is right and regardless of what reasons they may provide. By extension and for clarity, this idea also includes progressive income taxation and antipoverty programs derived from, or for, either persons or business.

Hank Rearden and Taggart demonstrate the other side of this paradigm. As they both struggle to produce by ethical means, they are continually pulled back by the leaches who both impede their ability to move forward and drain them of their monetary abilities to better execute production. Via frivolous laws, taxation and antipoverty programs, both Rearden and Taggart struggle to keep their companies alive. In essence, they are the well from which the other characters draw their life giving water, but without consent, restraint, or even the ability to moderate either the rate or perceived necessity of the pull.

Though often attributed to Alexander Tytler or Ben Franklin, it has been repeated throughout the years that when people discover that they can simply vote for the candidates that will give them money, it will herald the end of a republic. In the United States, we are guaranteed a Republic style of government. The Republic of course, arguably the fairest form of governance which secures the ability to be self-reliant, engage in commerce, and acquire happiness with limited restriction. However, Kenyen Brown, United States Attorney for the Southern District of Alabama references witticism when stating that *"the Constitution only gives people the right to pursue happiness. You have to catch it yourself"* (Brown, 2002). Powerful words that mirror the overall theme of people like Hank Rearden, Dagny Taggart, and for that matter, Ayn Rand.

That being said, it should be known that Atlas Shrugged is not the celebration of business. Instead, it is the celebration and recognition of labor, ingenuity, innovative thought, and self-reliance through ethical means. A definition of business is the practice of making one's living by engaging in commerce. Arguably the most effective way to engage in commerce is by understanding or controlling the means in which you engage in it as well as being the producer of the products or services you bring to exchange. If you profit from this but are not a contributor to this endeavor, you are merely a looter or a leach. However, the business community and hardworking freedom loving people do themselves a disservice by merely addressing it like that.

The wider theme of the novel seems to be an attempt to define exactly what people like James Taggard, Orren Boyle, and Wesley Mouch really are, or perhaps better said, are not. Who are people who engage in business, who have acquired power, esteem, and status, but who merely sponge off of true producers and provide little to no significant additions to the endeavor? Ayn calls these people "*looters*", the plunderers of business. They take revenue and means forcibly and unethically, and without the right to do so. Is this not theft as demonstrated earlier?

If Hank and Dagny are honest businessmen, then James and Orren are "*dishonest anti-businessmen*" because they are the opposite of the ideals, motives, efforts, and actions of Hank and Dagny. Though, perhaps the terms "*looter*" or "*anti-businessmen*" are not strong enough. It remains clear that people like James only commit to the creativity in which they can further drain the well before them. By basic definitions, they are thieves, or perhaps the epitome of true villains. However, if we are to recognize the actions and motives of people such as Rearden and Dagny as heroic, we must recognize James and Orren for what they are. After all, what do you call something that lives solely by deriving their benefits at a host's expense?

A parasite.

The Pursuit of Profit

It was recently mentioned to me that "*In today's world there is a growing segment of our society who view profits as wrong, as evil. Corporations, companies and others who pursue the profit motive are often considered mean, selfish, and unethical because it takes advantage of workers and the less fortunate.*" This statement was then followed up with the question of whether not pursuing profits is ethical.

We must address both points within the question as they are vital in understanding the true position. There is indeed a growing segment that sees profits as wrong, however this can be correlated to another interesting statistic which is also on the rise. We are witnessing an increase in those who favor socialism as well, and I believe the growing segment that this person addressed is the same one I am referring to. I also believe these ideas of profit being unfair or wrong to be interlaced with socialism as they tend to be the driving battle cries for it.

Both liberal Democrats and those aged 18-29 have showed strong growth in their support for socialism according to the Pew Research Center (Carrol, 2011). According to their research, today a strong majority of liberal Democrats support socialism and those aged 18-29 show an even greater shift toward favoring it. Considering the parties involved, I immediately suspect state run institutions of higher learning as a cause because these two classifications tend to go hand-in-hand.

For clarity, socialism is basically a political and economic theory of social organization that advocates that the means of production, distribution, and exchange should be owned or regulated by the community as a whole. In other words, "*a socialist economic system is a system of production and distribution organized to directly satisfy economic demands and human needs, so that goods and services are produced directly for use instead of for private profit driven by the accumulation of capital.*"

If we did not have to contend with the "*human factor*", it might sound nice, but this idea has a much darker side that is often either not taught to the 18-29 crowd, or simply ignored by all suspect parties. Once again, according to Marxist theory, socialism is a transitional social state between the overthrow of capitalism and the realization of communism. If anyone would know this, it would be Karl Marx.

To those who support socialist ideas, I often present the following question: "*Which communist state would you wish to live in? N.Korea, China, Cuba?*" History has shown time and time again, that this idea is a failure and one to avoid at all costs, if not simply destroy once realized in your own society. Why? Because historically speaking, it is an economic cancer. Even Vladimir Putin (then Russian Prime Minister and current President of Russia) suggested that the United States learn from Russian history and NOT exercise "*excessive intervention in economic activity and blind faith in the state's omnipotence*"; IE: Socialism (Putin, 2009).

The point in all of this is simply that socialism and communism are interlaced. In addition, these have also shown themselves to be highly ineffective in the long-term. At the same time, these ideals suggest what the person mentioned above was talking about in that they view profits as wrong and evil, and those corporations, companies and others who pursue the profit motive are mean, selfish, and unethical.

On the other hand, capitalists and many Americans (for the most part) embrace the idea of profit. Specifically, we tend to embrace a financial gain. We strive to increase the difference between the amount we earn and the amount we spend, be it in our homes, operating a business, or producing something.

It is the old battle between Keynesian economics and Austrian economics. One appears to only work in ideal circumstances, while the other appears to work in reality. That being said, we are asked if it is ethical to pursue profit. Well, is it ethical to pursue an increase in your means? It is ethical to expect a raise for loyalty and hard work? Is it ethical to be in a position of security if an emergency arises? It is ethical to have savings for retirement or school or perhaps even acquire something nice for yourself or the family? Finally, is it ethical to take an idea, start a business and provide jobs for those who seek work and who also wish for those things listed here? These are the things that profit can bring.

Is it ethical to pursue profits? The logical answer is an absolute *"yes"*. The pursuit of profit is very much ethical, but also a direct contrast with socialist ideas.

Profit is supposed to be a reward. Perhaps it is HOW one goes about acquiring that profit that should be ethically scrutinized.

A Lesson from Gandhi

The life of Gandhi, and for that matter his quests, are often subject to scrutiny, wonderment, and amazement due in large part to cultural differences, influences, life experiences, and happenstance. Some with Western philosophies may find it hard to imagine all of the different pieces that came together to make a timid, shy, and unsure person a national hero, leader, and treasure (Bondurant, n.d.).

One must remember a basic premise when evaluating Gandhi, which is that you can really only push someone so many times before they get tired of being pushed. Much of Gandhi's life was under the thumb of the British Empire. He was educated in London, fascinated by the life of the *"gentleman"*, and even tried to emulate the British for a time (Jackson & Gutknecht, 2001). He was loyal, but like a dog. Ironically, he eventually saw that he, along with his countrymen were treated as such (Biography, 2004). One can only imagine the revelations one could have had when coming to this realization. Ideas of true liberty begin to show their face, and in turn, it is usually only a matter of time before they are acted upon.

However, Gandhi is an exception in many ways, especially when we consider how liberty has been achieved the world over. Gandhi's methods were unique but still quite effective. Yet, it can almost be confusing how one so set on achieving liberty can also be an advocate for interdependence. The two concepts of liberty and interdependence are often portrayed as mutually exclusive, (IE: democracy vs communism) but that is because most people look upon philosophical ideas such as these as simple or one sided. It makes sense that Gandhi would be able to bridge these two ideas.

Liberty is a concept most are at least familiar with. It is the basic philosophy that identifies the condition to which an individual has the right to behave according to one's own personal responsibility and free will. Generally speaking, most people believe this to be a fundamental human experience anymore. During the time of Gandhi though, only a select few around the world enjoyed such freedoms. In this case we speak of the British, the oppressors of India and South Africa. Of course, it does not take a man of great insight to see that this is fundamentally wrong. Gandhi recognized that as individuals, we are born free and that our only masters or monsters to conquer should be ourselves. Gandhi once said "*The only tyrant I accept in this world is the 'still small voice' within me*" (Gandhi M., The essential gandhi: An anthology of his writings on his life, work, and ideas., 2002).

The world does not operate by the hands of one man alone, even Gandhi understood this. Gandhi once said "*Interdependence is and ought to be as much the ideal of man as self-sufficiency. Man is a social being. Without interrelation with society he cannot realize his oneness with the universe or suppress his egotism. His social interdependence enables him to test his faith and to prove himself on the touchstone of reality*" (Gandhi M., Young India., 1929). This is reminiscent of Rousseau's statement that "*Man is born free, and everywhere he is in chains*" (Rippey, 2001). Both are highly socialistic or communistic ideas. It would seem as though Gandhi understood that as a society, we are bound by one another. As creatures, we do often operate in "*packs*". As a family, we are stingy and collective, perhaps even overly proud.

Perhaps the mesh came with his Western influenced education that gave him insight into basic American ideas that we are all born with certain unalienable rights but that we need one another in order to secure these rights. One can only speculate the inner workings of Gandhi.

Historically speaking, securing such freedoms or liberties comes at a cost. It has often been said that freedom is not free. Gandhi, being a perpetual learner, more than likely understood this as the world has shown us that such liberties are usually paid for by the blood of those willing to secure them. It is the sacrifice of those who are principled that buy the liberties that are often enjoyed by the meek. Perhaps Gandhi wanted to change that.

Gandhi's struggles had to be non-violent for the purpose of winning over his followers as well as the world. Perhaps he understood that a great many people were by nature non-violent but that they still wanted to be involved. Perhaps it was a strategic measure on his part to gain the support from citizens across the world witnessing what was unfolding. Or perhaps, when referencing Gandhi's study of the Bible, we find he sought to echo the Christians in the coliseum who simply accepted their fate of martyrdom (Jackson & Gutknecht, 2001). Regardless, the tactic worked and yes, people got hurt and even killed, however the number could have been, and more than likely would have been much higher had combat ensued. Had Gandhi not recognized the limits of his movement or the brute strength and capabilities of the British, or had he simply sought a violent revolution, he could have had his people slaughtered in mass.

Thankfully, this was not the case for Gandhi or his people. In many ways, this is due to Gandhi's ability to capture the power of symbolism and his ability to share that vision with the world. Of course, humans often see symbols even when there are none to see. One could argue that Brigadier-General Reginald Dyer's order to massacre the Indians at Jallianwala Bagh or even the imprisonment of Gandhi any of the numerous times was symbolic (Jackson & Gutknecht, 2001). I think it is important for leaders to actively engage in manipulating symbolism for the favor. It is how people remember things. It is how people respond. People simply associate better with symbols. This is evident by the multi-billion dollar advertising industry that tries desperately to implant logos into our brains. Furthermore, even if a leader does not actively engage in this practice, it should be understood that people are going to pull out their own symbolism if it is not provided.

The story of Gandhi is striking in many ways, but none more so than the fact that his idea simply had never been tried before. In fact, there was not even a word for it until Gandhi created one. "*Truth (satya) implies love, and firmness (agraha) engenders and therefore serves as a synonym for force. I thus began to call the Indian movement Satyagraha, that is to say, the Force which is born of Truth and Love or non-violence, and gave up the use of the phrase "*passive resistance*", in connection with it, so much so that even in English writing we often avoided it and used instead the word "*satyagraha*" itself or some other equivalent English phrase*" (Gandhi M. K., 1928). As we can clearly see, any other method would have simply gone against what his core beliefs were. Being a man of principle, one would be hard pressed to imagine any other method being employed.

This tells us a lot about true and effective leadership. For starters, it illustrates that sometimes leaders have to forge a new path altogether, rather than to lead everyone down a road with known and often negative consequences. It shows us that leaders have to be willing to take a leap of faith first before they can expect others to make the same leap. Finally, it demonstrates that sometimes there is a better way, even when we do not see it right away. Perhaps discipline is the key word we need to utilize here. Remaining steadfast to the plan when we believe it to be the right way. This is often where one might debate the resolute dedication of leaders such as Barack Obama, however the plan and or path is the Constitution, to which we are obviously not following. The job of a leader is not always a great one. Hard decisions must be made. New ideas must be forged. The world is watching. Who is the leader?

In the end, there are many aspects of Gandhi's leadership that are applicable to, and useful in our own leadership practices and studies. As mentioned before, being willing to forge down uncharted territory is a great place to start. Innovative ideas and concepts are a must but they must originate from somewhere, they must be accepted and laid out by leadership, and they must be pursued by everyone. This could also mean merely accepting the ideas of a follower and rolling with it if you truly believe in it. The key is *"belief"*. Nothing can truly happen without that. Belief however, comes from understanding of the goal. You cannot truly believe in the Constitution for example, if you have not read it. You cannot be a real Christian, if you do not know the doctrine.

Other great examples could be remaining dedicated to a resolution or solution no matter how long it takes or what kind of hardships one must endure. One could also argue that Gandhi's life-long learning and improvement was vital in his success. He was always trying to improve himself and this was admired. Looking at everyone as equals, or listening to others are yet more great examples. Finally, simply being open-minded when it comes to the barriers we face and the solutions we could apply. With all this, if someone were to merely apply half of what has been covered and be only half as principled as Gandhi, you would still have a very effective leader on your hands. Perhaps his level of commitment alone is something to strive for.

That being said, it should be recognized that in today's world, there are aspects of Gandhi's style that would not be workable other than in very limited contexts such as in religious settings. A good example of this would be attempts at hunger strikes. In great part, this method works only if the opposing party cares. Another issue would be in that he dictated how and when people could communicate with him. For instance, Gandhi's weekly day of silence (Biography, 2004). One could only imagine what reaction the President might receive if he had a weekly day of silence where he was unable to speak. Most of the weaknesses come about or over Gandhi's personal initiatives. Not to say that constant refinement is not necessary for a leader, but I do not believe that in the Western philosophy, Corporate America, or government in general, such practices would be tolerated for long.

However, the study of Gandhi is important in many ways. To begin with, it illustrates the possibilities of will power, intestinal fortitude, drive, and above all else, what can happen when you are truly committed to your goals. In many ways, we could also say that it provides insight into the realm of "*what if*". It could also be argued that the story of Gandhi could be a road map for those who find themselves to be timid, or reserved. That perhaps one need not be an extrovert to change the world or even their surroundings.

Finally, every aspect of what one could learn from Gandhi could very much be utilized in the initial stages of course correction. As we discussed earlier, it is the symbolism of the figure that we must pull in order to make the coloration. The Constitution, the Founders, our Monuments, etc. We are not at war yet but we begin to engage in passive resistance to bad ideas or unconstitutional behaviors. We must constantly refine ourselves and navigate the turbulent waters of tyranny being handed down. We must hold our tongues at times as it is often best not to speak because our actions will speak louder than words.

Maybe in regard to leadership in the months and years ahead, the life and struggles of Gandhi are best summed up as analogies. While I feel as though this does a tremendous disservice to the life of Gandhi, we must also recognize that times are very much different, and that most people simple do not have a fraction of the self-discipline or principle that Gandhi did.

Maybe that is the problem. Maybe that is the place to start. At the very least, the lesson is to be resolved and see it through, no matter what. You may find yourself in a leadership position soon enough. What are you going to do when you are in it?

Does Race or Gender Make the Leader?

There are many different definitions of *"Leadership"*. Of course these vary dramatically depending on whom you are asking and in what context you may be referring. They all have common themes, but when diversity within leadership becomes the focal point, and when a spotlight on the uncontrollable physical attributes of an individual somehow becomes relevant to their ability to lead; the definitions of leadership can become contorted and become worthless altogether.

Forbes recently did a story entitled *"Top 10 Qualities That Make a Great Leader"*. The article presented qualities such as honesty, the ability to delegate, communication, a sense of humor, confidence, commitment, a positive attitude, creativity, intuition, and the ability to inspire as their top 10 (Prive, 2012). When searching other articles, both scholarly and media based, one finds much of the same. Still, in more than fifty articles searched, no mention of a single physical attribute was found to be necessary in regard to leadership ability. The question then becomes, why is this aspect ignored in definition if it is so important? Why do we not read that gender or race is as crucial to leadership as is the ability to communicate or delegate tasks? Is that because it would be considered racist or sexist? Is it because such a notion is ridiculous and an insult to intelligence? Perhaps. So how have we allowed such ideas to become acceptable? This in of itself has become a bigger issue than most are willing to even recognize.

To illustrate this point, we must consider James Burns' definition of leadership. Burns says that leadership is *"leaders inducing followers to act for certain goals that represent the values and the motivations—the wants and needs, aspirations and expectations—of both leaders and followers"* (Hickman, G. R., 1998). Notice that Burns didn't mention anything about color or gender. Burns made no mention of any attribute being an indicator of ability.

Perhaps it would be appropriate to look at a few other definitions of leadership before drawing a solid conclusion. Philip Gafka (2012), founder of leadership development firm Leap Associates says *"Leadership is employing your skills and knowledge, leveraged by your attitude to get the results you desire."* Robert Preziosi (2012), professor and past chairman of management at Nova Southeastern University's Huizenga School of Business says *"Leadership is actions committed by a person or group that produce an output or result. It simply helps people to get things done. It is not based on position in a hierarchy."* Jonas Falk (2012), a chef and the CEO of OrganicLife, a startup that provides nutritious school lunches says *"Leadership is the ability to take an average team of individuals and transform them into superstars. The best leader is the one who inspires his workers to achieve greatness each and every day."*

Numerous definitions of leadership and still not a word about a physical attribute. Once again, would such words be racist or sexist? The truth of the matter is that we are beginning to find that relating attributes to either criteria or definition in regard to leadership is not only wrong, but also dangerous and counterproductive.

An organization's main goal is to thrive. Common sense tells us that an organization cannot thrive without great leadership. As demonstrated, great leadership does not derive from skin tone or gender. The point is that if we collectively focus only on the diversity of the leadership of the group, all of the different definitions of leadership appear to be worthless. It is apparent that diversity is not the critical aspect when we look at the grand scheme of leadership.

The topic of slavery is usually where this conversation leads. We use this topic as an excuse to forcibly diversify our current institutions due to historical inequalities, while we (and history) try to forget the diversity of that institution's origination. The fact remains that in America, slave owners were comprised of both female and male individuals and that of African, Arabic, and European decent. Furthermore, slaves consisted of the very same sets. So we use slavery as an excuse while ignoring the fact that the real difference between slave and owner was really based out of the difference between the weak versus the strong, not of color or gender. This is a vital truth in this discussion.

Regardless of gender or color, the slave owners had an amazing ability to instill fear into their followers. The point is that leaders motivated their subjects out of fear, not color or gender. *"In fact, the oldest method of motivation is fear. Physical strength was originally the source of power, and weaker members of the group followed orders because they feared the physical punishment that was sure to result from refusal to conform"* (Strategic-Essentials, 2010). It was leadership in action, not affirmative action. The second point is that they were effective.

Some might debate whether a slave owner was a leader at all, instead of just cruel. This is a distraction method because by most definitions, we would have to concede that they were leaders. In the classic definition of the word, leadership is merely the action of leading a group of people or an organization. Burns even referenced the common definitions being *"leaders making followers do what followers would not otherwise do, or as leaders making followers do what the leaders want them to do"* (Hickman, 1998). Again, no references to physical attribute.

This is not a debate about shedding the social, gender, or racial inequalities of the past, or even how difficult that road has been. In fact, one could easily debate that the progress has been made. In January of 2010, more women than men were on payrolls according to US Labor Department statistics (Mulligan, 2010). As of June 2012, people of color made up 36 percent of the labor force (Burns, Barton, & Kerby, 2012). Setting aside the political discussion that usually follows such a statement, we should at least be able to concede that these are improvements. Still, these numbers do not reflect the point of leadership.

We must recognize that we do not have a choice in the gender or race we are born with. Still, we pretend that these attributes do not exist while at the same time, organizations are seeking these attributes to place within their ranks and trying desperately to show the world that they are diverse. Meanwhile, they continue to deny that such attributes even exist or influence their decisions. In some cases, this comes from law, in others it is merely for the perception of inclusion. However by passive participation in these practices, many organizations are suffering because instead of the best person for the position, they are filling positions for the sake of the physical attribute.

No doubt forced diversity has seen its victories, but it has also had its setbacks. Picking someone based purely off of physical attribute will more than likely land an organization someone with less than desirable qualities. In other words, being female or having a certain skin tone does not equate into having honesty, the ability to delegate, the ability to communicate, etc. This is a slippery slope anyway because when one is openly hired or fired based solely on certain physical attributes, it has the ability to be prosecuted as sexual harassment or discrimination. This is blatant hypocrisy by any measure.

The purpose of this chapter is not to seek answers, so much as better define the problem. I can concede to the idea that there are some organizations that would not be diverse had law not forced them into it, but the idea of forcing an organization to hinder its own processes for the sake of a physical attribute seems asinine. The result cannot possibly be a good one. For instance, forcing diversity at the National Black Chamber of Commerce (NBCC) seems counterproductive to their mission. While their organization and many others organizations like it could be considered racist organizations, forced diversity and affirmative action laws are not entirely needed because their intent is understood and somehow accepted by the majority.

Affirmative action was designed to ensure that an applicant's full background and life experience were considered as part of an admissions decision or hiring process (Kurland, 2012). Anyone could agree with this premise, but this is not what happened in practice. What happened was that often a less qualified person took the seat of a highly qualified person for the sake of diversity, not quality. This eventually took place on the leadership levels as well and the problems are becoming evident today. In fact, Gail Heriot, a member of the US Commission on Civil Rights and professor of law at the University of San Diego says that *"mounting empirical evidence that race preferences are doing more harm than good—even for their supposed beneficiaries."* She goes on to say that *"we now have fewer African-American physicians, scientists, and engineers than we would have had using race- neutral admissions policies. We have fewer college professors and lawyers, too. Put more bluntly, affirmative action has backfired"* (Heriot, 2013).

It is rather simple though. If a leader gets into position by physical attribute alone, the chances of having the "*wrong*" leader are probably pretty good. This is not a good situation for any organization considering where the organization might be led and for what reasons. If a leader is chosen based on attribute alone, could that leader be trusted fully? If the organization did not choose based on quality, will the decisions made by the leader be followed without question? Will that leader be followed at all? Long-term, what will happen to the leader who is constantly questioned or overridden because of the lack of trust or inability? What happens to the organization itself? All valid cause and effect questions that should be considered.

Understand of course, that there are many different positions within many organizations that can be forcibly diversified, but these are usually positions held by the followers. It is also recognized that there are key sectors of the workforce and in many organizations which lack diversity (Burns, Barton, & Kerby, 2012). For instance, we do not exactly see diversity on the board of the NAACP. These points are not in dispute. The point is that by any definition, we can clearly see that physical attributes play absolutely no role in the making of a great leader or their performance and therefore should in no way be required or considered when seeking a leader or describing one.

Perhaps the best way to say it would as follows: the term "*diversity in leadership*" should not be something sought so much as something appreciated. Or, better yet "*diversity in leadership*" should reflect the numerous qualities within the individual rather than the attributes they had no part in choosing. When we think of leadership, we should not see attribute, we should simply revere qualities.

If you value yourself as a leader, perhaps at least one of your duties should be in guiding people away from such ignorant thoughts and instead, turning such energies to the legitimate endeavor of fixing our broken system.

Racism and Sexism

Does the race or gender debate end with leadership? Of course not! There are some who try to state that any given race might be better than another. Better? In what regard? Or how about the women who somehow think that since they are female, they are somehow entitled to something above and beyond what men deserve?

Racism and sexism tend to derive out of ignorance. The unfortunate part is that the masses tend to be ignorant; hence the masses tend to be easily led into racism. It is sad really. Mixed with political correctness, this is a powder keg because few feel as though this can be an open topic. Racism and sexism are not just ignorant, they are stupid.

This idea becomes clear when you factor in other species into the debate. To watch people debate the merits of differences between a German Sheppard and a Basset Hound. Tell me why one should care about the gender or qualities of a Quarter Horse over a Paint. These are ideas based out of opinion and preference (at best) when at the end of the day, not a single animal being discussed had a choice in what they were, yet they still find themselves highly useful in regard to an overall purpose.

It should be clear; only racists see race and only sexists see gender. If you are offended by this statement, then this statement was written specifically for you. It is time you open your eyes to the bigger picture and stop being so unbelievably ignorant. You are missing out on so many amazing opportunities because you are holding yourself back over something horrible you have learned.

Sure, there are some who could rattle off a half a dozen statistics about certain abilities (either physical or mental) when it comes to the superiority of a certain race or the oppression of another. Do this with me and I can point just as many attributes that are less than appealing on you or shock you with an oppressed people you were unaware of.

These debates are once again, based out of a cultural value set provided by predecessors that may have no bearing, reference, or comparison to the cultural value system of the opposing race one may be comparing. Furthermore, as you will see in the following chapter, history that is currently taught is not a history that is accurate. This leads to confusion and the unknown which in turn breeds fear.

Some of the most cruel slave owners were black. Some of the most savagely beaten and killed in the slave trade were white. You were not aware? Many Scots/Irish were slaves and brutally beaten and murdered. So think about this: white and black slave owners, white and black slaves. But can you guess what people were ultimately responsible for the slave trade?

Ironically, there are many racists today who attempt to convert their followers to the religion most associated with slavery, on the premise of hating others who were just as much a victim of the slave trade. On the other side, racists recruit followers into an organization known for their racial hypocrisies and fundamentally flawed ideology. This ignorance frustrates me.

Let us explore some real American history when it comes to slavery. The majority of slaveholders, white and black, owned only one to five slaves. More often than not, and contrary to what Hollywood would have you believe, slaves and masters worked and ate alongside each other, especially in the North.

Yes, there were some (like Washington) who owned quite a few slaves. Many are quick to bring up the founders as though they were scum for having participated in the practice. Once again, public education has failed you. Here is quote from George Washington: "*I can only say that there is not a man living who wishes more sincerely than I do to see a plan adopted for the abolition of slavery.*"

Twelve of the Founding Fathers owned or managed slave-operated plantations or large farms: Bassett, Blair, Blount, Butler, Carroll, Franklin, Jefferson, Jenifer, Madison, Mason, Charles Pinckney, Charles Cotesworth Pinckney, Rutledge, Spaight, and Washington. This is often taken out of context though because the economic model is so misunderstood today.

For instance, Thomas Jefferson owned inherited slaves. However it is rumored that he had children with one of his "slaves". In October, 1802, while he was president, there was a story that was published in the newspapers that Thomas

Jefferson was keeping one of his wife's slaves, Sally Hemings, as a concubine and was producing children from her. Jefferson, who lived for 44 years after the death of his wife and who never remarried, never denied the story. Of the children he is said to have had, all were freed.

Something many today are simply unaware of is the idea that people could buy their freedom during that time. During this country's period of slavery, many freed blacks worked for years to purchase the freedom of family members. You would be shocked to learn of just how many freed slaves became slave masters themselves and for the same reason as whites, simply to make use of slave labor so that they could make more money. It was simply more economical and there is not a single race immune from the responsibility of the practice and few that were not also victims.

It should also be noted that only about five percent of the over ten million black slaves to be transported to the Western Hemisphere, actually made it to what is now known as the United States. The vast majority of the rest were dropped off and sold in what is now the Caribbean and South America. That means that the rest of the black population came to the United States via their own free will. Here again, the Arabs were still trading slaves long after the United States abolished the practice. In fact, slavery wasn't abolished in Saudi Arabia until 1962.

The point is that there is not a single race at fault here. To begin with, it was black Africans and Muslims who rounded up other blacks from other tribes in order to sell them to whites who bought them. Muslims were and are encouraged to live in the way of Muhammad, who was a slave owner and trader. The whites used versus from the Bible to justify slavery with passages such as Ephesians 6:5 and Titus 2:9. As a matter of fact, Muslims began large-scale buying and selling of African slaves 600 years before Europeans did and continued to do so 100 years after.

Regardless, slavery was bad. Blacks were wrong, whites were wrong, the Muslims were wrong. We all know it. The descendants of the slaves and the owners need to get over it at some point. Not all white people had slaves. Not all black people came from slave families and not all Muslims are responsible.

One of the more humorous examples of racial idiocy is that of the Nazi's. According to the Nazis' racist ideology, Arabs are racial Semites and thus sub-humans, similar to Jews. Yet, Hitler aligned himself with Amin Al Husseini and Muslims due to common goals. Another example of how public education has failed you, Hitler provided for an SS Muslim Hanzar Division of which Amin Al Husseini was head of. For clarity purposes, these were not people considered Aryan, and they were not German.

So today, due in large part to this ignorance, many black Americans turn or convert to Islam (known for their collaboration with the Nazi's and their responsibility of slavery during the 1600-1800's) to counter what they deem to be racial inequality by whites. Why? Because of the ignorant things they have learned from other ignorant people and due in large part to the many things they have NOT learned.

There are some who flat out hate white people for any number of reasons. Once again, this is based out of ignorance. Not all whites can be grouped together. There are pretty substantial differences between the different groups such as Celtics, Normans, Saxons, etc.

Let me provide you a side note for consideration. To further this idea let me say that even the most educated racists are still rather ignorant. For instance, many racists will have you believe that people of different religious sects are considered a "*race*", such as the "*Jews*". Judaism is not a race. There are some even within the Jewish community who even think they are a race, but this simply cannot be true. You cannot convert into a race and a race cannot be comprised of numerous other races. For clarity purposes and for instance, there are black Jews, none more famous than the Jews in the African diaspora who actually believe they are the original sect. It should also be noted that there is a huge difference between the Jewish and the Zionists.

An understanding of REAL history will help people clear up some of these basic misconceptions, which of course schools seem to refuse to teach. Another great example would be the concept of "*anti-Semitic*". How many people do you know that sling hateful words at Arabic or Syriac people but cry "*anti-Semitic*" when anything negative is said about the Jewish or the government of Israel? This is due to ignorance. For clarity and to reiterate, Arabic and Syriac people are also Semitic.

On a similar note, just because one disagrees with a government action, does not mean that this person is a racist. One can in fact dislike what President Obama stands for and not be a racist against his half-black status. One can in fact dislike what the government of Israel does and not be "*anti-Semitic*" for disliking that action. Black Americans were justified in their frustration and hatred for Democrats because they simply refused to do anything about Civil Rights, because the Democrats were in fact acting in a racist manner.

Regardless, some may read this chapter and find themselves thinking that the information is nice but that racism will always exist, due in large part to pride. Pride for your heritage is one thing. Hate for another is an entirely different thing altogether.

There is legitimate hate, and moronic hate. Legitimate hate would be against someone who undermines basic human Rights such as the Constitution of the United States. Racism is moronic hate. Sexism is moronic hate. You should be proud of your heritage. Of course, that requires actually knowing it. The idea is to learn. It is rather simple, and if you follow the advice provided, you will notice your circle of friends probably decreasing in number while at the same time diversifying. You will eliminate the ignorant from your life, and you will be better for it.

Race is not an issue unless you let it be. Genetically, you can find greater differences between two frogs than you can between any two races. In people, the difference is near 0.1%. The true difference derives out of the ideas in the heads of those who either think or do not think. Not the color, not the gender.

Race is not the issue . . . radical religion and power mongers are the issues. More irony, these are the very same groups encouraging you to hate someone else. Funny how that works.

Leaders who continually turn every problem into a race problem or a gender problem only help to perpetuate the problems we face. This is what is known as finding a scapegoat. It means finding a distraction and blaming a set of problems on that distraction even though there really is no reason for the blame.

So who should we hate? It is just an opinion, but we should probably collectively and aggressively hate anyone trying to advance power of the government over the people, anyone who supports our enemies, (foreign or domestic), anyone seeking to establish global government that supersedes our sovereignty, or anyone who attempts to destroy or infringe upon our Constitutional Rights. Maybe we should hate those who seek to keep important information from the minds of those who seek or need it. Once again, there is legitimate hate, and then there is moronic hate; I hope you are beginning to see the difference.

Do not get side tracked. We can either unite on the basis of being American, or we will collectively watch this nation fall apart. It empowers government to have you divided. As a matter of fact, the argument can be made that the organization responsible for exacerbating the race and gender divide is the Federal Government.

That may be hard to imagine for some, but let me again provide you with another blaring example of how this works.

A 600-plus page manual used by the military to train its Equal Opportunity officers was recently obtained by Fox News. This manual teaches that *"healthy, white, heterosexual, Christian"* men hold an unfair advantage over other races, and warns in great detail about a so-called *"White Male Club."*

"Simply put, a healthy, white, heterosexual, Christian male receives many unearned advantages of social privilege, whereas a black, homosexual, atheist female in poor health receives many unearned disadvantages of social privilege," reads a statement in the manual created by the Defense Equal Opportunity Management Institute (DEOMI) (Starnes, 2013).

However, this happens in the schools too on all levels. A brief example: Duke University professor Eduardo Bonilla-Silva says the US is *"not post-racial,"* and claims minorities are still being mistreated on a scale comparable to the 1960s, though modern whites have cleverly disguised their racism. In his opinion, a Caucasian's embrace of inclusion and tolerance is actually proof of his or her hatred of non-whites (Agee, 2013).

We must stop this. We do not need more government to end it because it is government who has allowed it and often times made it worse. We need to find it in ourselves to be kind and open to those who are different from ourselves. You hold the key, but remember: only those who see race can be racists. Stop seeing differences and seek out what connects us.

A Lack of Education

Undoubtedly, much of the information in this book will be new for most. Still, a few may have been exposed to at least some of it at some point. This begs the question; *"Why weren't we taught this stuff in school and why I don't I hear this more?"*

This chapter is not a blanket statement either. There are going to be some reading this that attended private school, or who were home schooled, or perhaps went to public school but then went to a private college. Of course, there are also those who have were victims of public school but were lucky enough to have been awaken and researched much of it all themselves. Understand that this chapter is not about ALL education per say, instead it is a focus on government-run education.

Knowledge is power right? This is often why you will hear me say that the nation as a whole has been rendered powerless. The majority of schools in the country today are dictated, at least in some part, by the government. This usually comes by way of curriculum. This is no secret. We need to stop right there though do we not? There are some who would like to retort with the idea that education is run by the individual states. True, this used to be the case, but since the inception of programs such as *"Race to the Top"*, or the No Child Left Behind Act, can we really say that? What about when we consider the Common Core State Standards Initiative?

A great example of just how bad it has become, is the idea that the President of the United States has the power to create laws or "*get stuff done*". Everyone these days looks to the President to solve all of their problems. However, if government-run education was worth a fraction of what was really paid, more people would probably know that the President of the United States CANNOT make laws, declare war, decide how federal money will be spent, interpret laws, or even choose Cabinet members or Supreme Court Justices without Senate approval. Did you even know this? Do not feel bad if you did not. You can place the blame squarely on the shoulders of the government who provided you the education. That being said, this is very good example of the unbelievably high level of ignorance in this country today.

Think about it, if knowledge is power then essentially, government (federal or states governments pandering the federal level) have provided you the power they wanted you to have. Another way to look at it could be to say that they have rendered you powerless. The information they provided seems to be just enough to get you through life, but not enough to really question their actions. After all, it would be pretty difficult to protest the trampling of a right if you do not know what that right is to begin with.

Have you ever wondered why English, Math, and Science were the focus? Sure, you are taught some social studies, a little history and maybe even a little government, but if you were asked to list the cabinet positions and who currently held those positions, could you do it? If you were asked to delineate the "*Intolerable Acts*", could you do it? How about defining the procedure of impeachment or how a law is created? Or more importantly, do you know how to repeal a law? How to go about running for an office? Perhaps you were not into these subjects.

What was Alexander Hamilton's connection to the Central Bank? What was the reason provided by Benjamin Franklin to fight the Revolutionary War? Why did we not read about Black Slave Owners or white slaves? Why is the Constitution not memorized? Why is the Bill of Rights not memorized? Perhaps you are just not interested in learning about colonial times? We could do this for days.

To really drive home the point, we have to look at an event that just about everyone is familiar with. Everyone knows about Lewis and Clark. Their expeditions were covered quite a bit in school. School plays, books, etc. Do you think it is weird then that you cannot remember hearing about the death of Captain Meriwether Lewis?

It is a simple equation my friends. Just like in the case of Captain Meriwether Lewis, if you knew all of the circumstance, you would ask questions and dig. If you dig, you will come across more things to question. With each new question comes a new answer. Each answer provides new insight until eventually you find the total truth. However, if that truth needed to be suppressed for any reason, the easy way to avoid all of the hassle is to simply not provide you information that you would question, and present related information at a time when you are not able to ask such high-level questions anyway. Like childhood.

It is not just grade school though. Let us look at high school or even college level ideas. Why does the United States celebrate Cinco-de-Mayo but not Mexico? What was the Act of 1871? What was Andersonville? Abraham Lincoln instituted Martial Law during the Civil War, who rescinded it? What is the Federal Reserve Act? What branch of government does the Federal Reserve fall under? What was the Bonus Army? Why did the US not bomb Tokyo? Why did the Japanese not advance onto the West Coast after having decimated the pacific fleet at Pearl Harbor? When did birth certificates start and why? What is Universal Commercial Code and how does it relate to the Constitution? Why was Operation Gunnerside so important? What is the Holocene extinction? What was the Kent State Massacre? This list goes on as well. Were you not interested in these facts either?

There is a ton of information that probably should have been taught, but was not. Ask yourself what seems more likely: these were not taught because of time constraints or, these were not taught because by learning these "*trivial*" facts, you will be able to see certain truths that some simply do not want you to know?

Think about all the things you did (or do) in school that are not exactly relevant in the grand scheme of your life, or are things you have yet to or will never really use. Is it substantial?

If knowledge is power, then there is information that empowers a populous and information that empowers the establishment. This is the paradigm in which we play. We send our children off to a government-run school, where they learn trivial ideas, mathematics, music, science, etc., but learn little of what really impacts their lives in regard to their own personal power. This is further skewed due to messages via bias or state-run media and pop-culture.

So what is the result? The US Department of Education's National Center for Education Statistics (NCES) recently released the initial results of an international survey of adult skills in literacy and mathematics, revealing that Americans rank 21st in "*numeracy*" and are tied for 15th in literacy among adults in 23 advanced economies (NCES, 2013). When we look deeper, we see that the Organization for Economic Co-operation and Development (OECD) did not put it so nice. They stated that the US fared badly in all three fields, ranking somewhere in the middle for literacy but way down at the bottom for technology and math (OECD, 2013). Is this why so many Americans do not understand the national debt, let alone their own?

Just about everyone has seen a Mark Dice video or a Late Night talk show video where someone on the street interviews an average American who is dumber than a bag of rocks. They sign petitions in favor of Nazi Police States, women sign petitions ending Suffrage, and of course many fail miserably when it comes to history in general.

Sure, you laugh at this, but it should scare you to death. Our math scores are low, our literacy is low, or comprehension of technology is low, and most people found history and government classes boring and were entirely disengaged, and you find humor in this? Is it really any wonder that the people of this great nation continue to fight over trivial ideas as though their lives depended on them? Laugh it up America.

I want you to think about this and what it probably means to you and your family. Ignorance is simply lacking knowledge or awareness in general; to be uneducated (ignorant, n.d.). If one does not have the information necessary to make a sound decision, they are easily led by those who appear to have the information needed. Are you easily led? Do you follow party lines just because? Do you do what you're told just because someone appears to be in a position of authority?

At some point it became cool to disregard an education. Nerds were frowned upon. The smart were shunned. Why? I remember hearing from classmates that the only reason they even went to school was because their parents made them go, as if being ignorant was something to strive for.

The answer and/or reason is found in three specific areas: their entertainment, the apathy of their parents, and a government-run education system. Please do not confuse this point. It is not the fault of the video games or the movies we watch per say, instead, it is the people and messages that children were allowed to idolize without direction. It is the parents who do not question their children's curriculum and do not take time at home to teach their children anything. Of course, I understand the difficulty of a parent being expected to do this considering most parents were "*educated*" in the same system. This is ignorance breeding ignorance by the way.

Seriously! How is identifying civilizations in North America during the pre- Columbian era going to help you? How is understanding the role of religion in regard to the growth and development of the United States really a relevant topic, especially when they REFUSE to cover Deism or Unitarianism? What about the Civil War? Why are they teaching it had anything to do with slavery?

Not only is an amazing amount of information NOT being taught, the information they are teaching is contorted to say very the least. Since we have focused on the Bill of Rights in this book, it seems only wise to demonstrate the point of this chapter using the very same.

In the book, "*United States History: Preparing for the Advanced Placement Examination*," which acts as a study guide for the Advanced Placement US history test, it says the following about the Second Amendment: "*The people have the right to keep and bear arms in a state militia*" (Newman & Schmalbach, 1998). Now, understand that this book also serves as a guide to accompany a year-long course in AP or honors US history. So they are literally changing history (books and all) and this is what will be considered "*honors US History*"? You should know that this is just one example of many.

If you have not figured it out by now, then let me be blunt: modern education is NOT education in the classical sense. Education by definition is an enlightening experience. I would imagine you have been more enlightened reading this book than you were during the entirety of your "*education*". Now, think about your kids, think about today's generation or even the next. We are in trouble because today's education "*standards*" amount to control, indoctrination and elimination of free thought. The reason Constitutional principles are slipping in this country is because they are not being taught at school or at home, and what is being taught at school (as demonstrated) is not exactly accurate.

There has been a deliberate "*dumbing down*" of the people in this great nation. It is not only obviously, but also extremely easy to demonstrate. If you make the mistake of trying to condone, explain, or excuse this atrocity, then you are aiding and abetting the enemy of your country. This practice of rendering the people stupid is unacceptable.

It is not just in certain subjects, it is in all subjects. This includes basic things like health. Did you know they teach that salt is bad for you even though salt is critical to your life? They teach that antibiotics are a good thing and that bacterium is bad. One almost has to laugh at the idea of having a "*health*" class that will not address cultured food or the words of Hippocrates. Of course no one thinks about the long-term effects or the chronic diseases that may come with such ideas. Hence, dumb Americans are becoming obese and sick in droves. Perhaps the goal is to allow the ignorant to kill themselves off.

It becomes just sad when the average person cannot assess potential dangers due to their unbelievable ignorance as well. All of the signs and labels stating what some would deem to be the obvious, all because there are people who simply cannot think.

A quick point in case: between 2004 and 2009, water suppliers across the US (public city water) detected 316 contaminants in water supplied to the public. The list of detected contaminants includes: 97 agricultural pollutants, including pesticides and chemicals from fertilizer—and manure-laden runoff; 204 industrial chemicals from factory discharges and consumer products; 86 contaminants linked to sprawl and urban areas or from polluted runoff and wastewater treatment plants; 42 pollutants that are byproducts of the water treatment processes or that leach from pipes and storage tanks (EWG, 2009). None of these are things that people would want to drink voluntarily.

The problem here is that the human brain is about 75% water. So those who drink from the tap in contaminated areas potentially feed their brains the very same water that has 316 contaminants in it. Can you imagine what this might do to brain function? Now, some can weigh the risks before tipping back the glass but many simply cannot. The point is not to make you want to stop drinking the water; the point is that many people simply cannot draw the correlation between cause and effect and this is primarily because they believe that since it is provided by the government, it has to be safe even though the evidence suggests otherwise. Why? Indoctrination. Perhaps the point is that people have lost the ability to think for themselves courtesy of the public school system.

Can we really be shocked though? Surely more people walked away from high school asking themselves "is that it?" Maybe this too should not be a surprise. After all, the teachers were not only produced in that system, they were also born out of that system, the very same system that teaches that the purpose of an education is for your career. What a joke! Perhaps none of us should be shocked at how dumb so many Americans really are.

So ask yourself the following questions:

What is Common Core?

Why do so many Private School kids and Home School kids seem so advanced?

We must stop pandering to the ignorant mass. Carry yourself as an intellectual and act accordingly. Be smart. Attempt to get smarter. Walk away from the morons.

For the religiously guided, I provide you the following: Proverbs 9:6-16 "*Leave the company of ignorant people, and live. Follow the way of knowledge.*"

The Three Rule Method

There have been several references to the *"Three Rule Method"* made throughout this book. Honestly, out of all of the words of wisdom I could probably provide, the Three Rule Method would more than likely be the most valuable.

The Three Rule Method is a technique I developed during college that allowed me to narrow down the best possible solution, in the shortest period of time, with greatest possibility of being correct.

As it turned out, with a little bit of practice, it was functional in many other areas besides just taking tests. I began to practice the method in almost all areas of life and found that more often than not, that it was extremely effective and highly accurate. I must stress however, that it takes practice and discipline because if you lie to yourself, the model cannot work.

To demonstrate this model, we will use the following statement: *"Thomas is a great guy, he throws the best parties. Come to Tom's house with me tonight!"*

Now, we apply the model which appears as follow: Basic Logic > Cause and Effect > and Occam's Razor.

Basic Logic: Use your best critical thinking skills to evaluate and/or separate truth from falsehood, or the reasonable from unreasonable beliefs. You need to identify the topic at hand, ensure it does not contradict truth, and finally, ensure truth based on whatever additional information you can find that is not readily presented. This could include your own personal memory or any other clues you might be able find. In this step, it is usually best to eliminate *"feelings"* or *"emotions"* when evaluating the topic.

Example:

Basic logic tells us only that Thomas is a male, he is known for throwing parties, and the person asking the question is obviously going tonight. We do not know if Thomas is really a great guy or a serial killer. We do not know if the only reason he is considered a great guy is because he throws great parties or buys everyone drinks. These other pieces of information are really just opinions. What if you do not like parties? What if you do not like to drink? What if the parties really are not that great?

Cause and Effect: A cause is WHY something happens. An effect is WHAT happens due to that cause. In this phase, compile multiple possible solutions without bias. From the reasonable to the unreasonable. This step is vital because it allows you to consider the un-considerable without feeling guilty for exploring what you would otherwise ignore. Then, you evaluate possible outcomes for each answer as a possible solution.

Example Cont:

Option 1—Thomas is in fact a serial killer. If I go tonight, I will die a horrible death after he executes a drug facilitated sexual assault on me having spiked my drink with Rohypnol.

Option 2—I will go to the party, meet someone special and spend the rest of my life in bliss. I have to go because if I do not, I will miss out on the best years of my life.

Option 3—Thomas is really only considered a nice guy because he buys everyone drinks. He is really just a lonely guy with few real friends. He is probably a pompous Ass but if I avoid him, I may have a good time and the drinks will be free anyway.

Option 4—My friend is going to the party, so Thomas cannot be too bad. And if something does start to get out of hand, I have my friend there to help keep an eye on things. And who knows, I might meet some new friends.

Option 5—My friend is always right about everything. Thomas is a great guy and I should do exactly what my friend says.

Occam's Razor (or Ockham's razor): This is an old philosophy that states that among competing hypotheses, the hypothesis with the fewest assumptions should be selected. In other words, do not over multiply; do not assume aspects that are not already present. All things being equal, the simplest answer is probably the right one.

Example Cont:

So now that you have some options, you get to make a decision. Once again, while evaluating your possibilities, you are using logic, not emotional bias such as fear. Occam's Razor aids in the selection. In the example provided, Thomas is probably not a serial killer. Your friend seems to like him and you like your friend. Thomas may actually be a jerk but your friend will be there with you. No one is perfect but you might actually enjoy yourself. So, the best option is probably going to be Option 4.

Understand that what you have done is used your brain to effectively make a prediction several hours in the future. Granted, many people make decisions like this every day without giving it this much thought. So imagine what you could do if you did make the effort and practiced the steps.

I have used this method very effectively throughout the years. As I practiced it more and more, I began to realize that instead of just projecting hours, or day, one could project months and sometimes even years if provided enough evidence to consider.

I was asked once what I saw in the years ahead regarding the United States. With my understanding of the cycles already presented in this book, and with my Three Rule Method already well-practiced, I decided to see if *"long-term projection"* was a possibility. I had to tweak the model but sure enough, it is almost as simple as the first model and again, it is highly accurate if the information you put into the model is sound.

The model however cannot account for alterations in decisions. It should be noted that when dealing with projections, it is a "*best guess*" based on the information currently available. I would also recommend quarterly reevaluations of the information in the model to ensure the integrity of the projection.

In order to look longer term, you need to add in a few steps. The model then appears as follows:

Basic Logic > Cause and Effect > Occam's Razor > Cause and Effect > Basic Logic > Occam's Razor

In other words, take your first conclusion and apply cause and effect to get even more solutions, then reapply basic logic, and then choose the best answer out of the new options.

Let me use the cycles presented earlier in this book as an example. We know that nations rise and fall. We know that every time a nation falls, there are certain factors present. The United States has many of the factors presented. We also know that nothing lasts forever. So, based on the Three Rule Method, we know that the United States will fall at some point. But when? We must add more information to the model.

Using the cycles, we can see that every 60 to 80 years, there is an economic upheaval and a big war. We know that our current time falls within cycles presented and we recognize that our economic situation is in fact, in the toilet. History shows us that nations fall by economic collapse, by war, or by both. We know that we are towards the end of Tytler cycle as well. We also know that all of the cycles presented are aligning in what appears to be some kind of perfect storm. If you are reading this book, you know the reality of the situation. So, the model tells us that we are actually at high risk currently. It is not to say that it is a guarantee that we will collapse. But again, we have to remember that there has never been a nation with a fiat currency that did not end in the collapse of the currency and the economy that held it.

This model, this theory, is not the final word on the topic. The bigger question is what does the model tell you? What are your conclusions?

Part 5 – Moving Forward

What Can I do?

There are many who have already decided that there is not a single thing in the world they can do about the corruption or the inevitable. The truth of the matter is that nothing could be further from the truth. There is actually quite a bit you can do, you just need to change the perception of what needs to be dealt with. Imagine our situation as an airplane going down. Will you survive? Is there anything you can do? What should you do? Sure, you feel helpless, but the reality is that what you do now can make all the difference.

First, you need to square yourself away. Put your oxygen mask on; make sure you are buckled in tight. Then, you can start worrying about those around you. If the opportunity presents itself, you may be able to go help fly the plane or merely help others escape the burning wreckage. You see, it is all about perspective. You just have to own the options presented. There is nothing you can do about the plane going down. That has already been decided.

You have power; you just need to exercise that power. If you choose to marginalize that power, that is on you, but it does not mean that power does not exist. I hope you read each item and really consider each point, because you will be amazed at how effective each point can really be.

Can you change history? Can you change the government's actions? Can you change the financial system? Can you personally repeal each frivolous law? Of course not.

Bigger steps like that come with time and tenacity. Sometimes it is only after the wreck that we can find the flaw that took us down. However, just because it cannot be changed today, does not mean we ignore it because we know it can be changed in the long run. So what about right now? Let us look at some of the things that you can do about our current situation.

The very first thing you need to do is read the Declaration of Independence and the Constitution in a single setting. That way, you will never be asking someone else to do something you have not already done. Do NOT be a hypocrite.

Then, you need to memorize your Bill of Rights or at the very least, the general idea of each. Hopefully this book helped in that. (This is not hard)

Teach your children (if you have them) or other family members about Constitutional Principles. In our family, we talk about such things on the 4th of July. This helps them understand the reason we celebrate it and gives the adults a reason to read the documents continually. It is also great for question and answer sessions.

Embrace the idea that the nation that we see today will not be the nation we see tomorrow. While our principles will live on, the nation will more than likely not look anything like it does today, just as it looks nothing like it did even a generation ago.

Start participating in passive resistance. Essentially, this means opposing the government without using violence, especially by refusing to obey laws that are unconstitutional. It is noncooperation. Why should you adhere to laws which unconstitutional? Is it not your duty to resist such activities?

Become vocal to friends and family members about unconstitutional laws. Bad mouth the idea that these laws could even exist. Keep the statements short, and repeat them often.

Stop filling your head with trash television. This includes the mainstream media. Remember, all things in moderation.

Start paying attention to local, national, and world events. You do not have to know everything about everything, but have a clue about what is going on.

Utilize more than one source for your news and information. If you continue to get your news or information from the same source, you will not have the ability to question anything.

Employ the "*Three Rule Method*" in your evaluation of the news and information you review. Do not blindly accept anything as final until having done so.

Be prepared for disaster. The ASPCA, FEMA, the DHS, READY. GOV, the CDC, the Red Cross and so many more are telling people to be prepared for disaster. This is because of two primary reasons: 1) more than 200 million people are affected by disasters each year and 2) there is not a spot on the planet that is immune. Look at Katrina, Greensburg KS, Hurricane Sandy, 9/11, etc. Bad things CAN happen. Being prepared is crucial. Be ready for 3 days, 3 weeks, 3 months, or even 3 years, whatever you can do. Understand that whatever preparations you put together now, will put you miles ahead of the majority who are not. By being prepared, this will give you power.

Be prepared to defend yourself. We have seen countless examples over the last several years that demonstrate that police, fire, EMS, etc., can merely react, not prevent. With these agencies being reduced substantially due to budget cuts, it does not take a rocket scientist to figure out the result. You might remember the story of a woman from Josephine County Oregon, who was raped in her home after calling 911 and staying on the line for more than 10 minutes. She was told there were no officers available to help her and the best advice that 911 could offer was 'If he . . . assaults you, can you ask him to go away?'—Be prepared to defend your own life. By being prepared, this give you power.

Know and understand your principles. You cannot stand on your principles if you do not have any. Do not just think them . . . write them down so that you own them. Do not get lazy on this step.

Embrace the idea that if ANYONE opposes or infringes Constitutional Law or flat out ignores the Bill of Rights, they are not only an enemy to you, they are an enemy of the these United States. This includes ANYONE who was stupid enough to swear an oath they were/are not willing to adhere to.

Stop associating with friends or family who poison your mind. Understand that a great portion of this nation has already been drinking from the punch bowl. You will not be able to wake up many of them. For example: If someone can look you in the face and seriously try to justify why Bush was better than Clinton or why Bush was better than Obama or vice versa, then you have a seriously uninformed or misinformed person on your hands. So unless you are proactively trying to wake them up, avoid them. As demonstrated, there is the "*Left/Right*" side of the spectrum, and then there are those who see truth.

Network with like-minded people. This step is crucial, especially when the inevitable does occur. Be it a civil or global situation, it would behoove everyone to have a group of like-minded people with whom you could work with when the time comes.

Find even more like-minded people. This is fairly easy to do actually. All you have to do is stop being afraid to discuss things that really matter. It is that simple. Of course, there are communities full of like-minded people both physically and online. I would encourage you seek them out and remain there.

Start a group for like-minded people in your area. Get out and practice bushcraft skills together, go to the shooting range together, teach each other and build skill sets together. Involve the kids and demonstrate to the kids how these things are so important.

Teach your children about firearms and their necessity in our culture. Teach your kids about firearm safety. Do not allow the topic of firearms to become taboo with them. Get to your kids before someone else does.

Support like-minded events. Go to a rally, go to a book signing, go to a protest. This does a couple of things. To begin with, this is a show of force. Remember, activity breeds activity. The second thing is that by going you will find like-minded people that you will be able to network with. The key here is that you need to support your fellow patriots. Be ready to do so and follow through.

Share and distribute like-minded information. This book for instance, would make a great gift. This is especially true if you feel as though you know someone who on the verge of waking up. Do NOT be afraid to express your views and help others. By the way, if you are afraid of losing friends because of your views, then you really need a new set of friends anyway.

Take the time to blog, write notes, or simply post information and/or your commentary about unconstitutional actions. Be a voice of the resistance. Thinking it is one thing, but letting someone else know they are not alone can make all the difference in the world. Be brave, because you are not alone either.

Get your education from privately held conservative type institutions if at all possible. State-run education has failed. Do not frown upon homeschooling, celebrate it.

Practice your skills. If you shoot, practice. If you camp, practice. If you garden, practice. If you do not partake in activities such as these, then start. Learn to filter water. Learn to look for natural sources of food. Take your new like-minded friends and go practice together. This also aids in being prepared for disaster. You will be able to fend for yourself because you will know how to. In other words, what happens when your preparedness supplies run out and there is not a soul there to help you? Ask yourself how long the aftermath of a disaster might last.

I am not a financial advisor, but it stands to reason that if the threat of dollar collapse or hyperinflation is real, then perhaps hedging yourself against such events might be wise. Of course, it would also stand to reason that if the wealthy are asset rich and dollar slim, then perhaps this too lends credibility to idea of owning assets. A great way to do this is by owning silver and/or gold (in my opinion). Now, there are those who will debate this, but I do not really validate their argument because there are a couple things I know for sure: all fiat currencies fail and gold and silver have never been worth zero. Simple enough.

While I ask you to embrace the cycles and prepare for the worst, I also want you to realize that it will not be the end of the world. Just like before, the war and the economic hardships will pass. There will be better times in the future just like there was before. You do not need to get down or depressed or ignore the facts, you need to embrace them and plan accordingly so that you and your family can survive and thrive on the other side.

Embrace the Republic. Memorize what it means so that you can pass it on easily to someone else.

Understand and spread the idea that the true power is NOT on the Federal level. Understand that pursuant to the 10th Amendment that the powers not entrusted to the United

States specifically by the Constitution, nor prohibited by it to the States, are reserved to the States respectively, or to the people. You have the power, act like it. Of course, this is yet another reason why you MUST read the Constitution, so you are fully aware of the power you really have. When you vote, vote ONLY for those who embrace the Republic. You do NOT want someone who believes we live in a Democracy and will not listen to their constituents. Focus on the state. Elect a strong like-minded Governor. Remember, the states can circumvent Congress.

Understand that freedom is not free. You may have to actually fight or support the fight in some way shape or form. You have to understand that whether you like it or not, you are a part of a time that will be studied and pondered for hundreds, if not thousands of years. You have the ability to be a part of forming what these events end up being, or hiding allowing something horrible to occur. I am challenging you to take a stand.

Stop giving your money to corporations that either support or defend unconstitutional actions. Can this be inconvenient at times? Of course, but this goes back to your principles. If you give your money to such corporations, then you literally have no business complaining about their activities.

Support only the companies with a common goal or who simply support the Constitution. This can become complex and may require a bit of research on your part. For example: if you oppose socialized medicine, so stop buying GMO foods from the companies who have the favor of the government. GMO foods eventually make you sick, which gives more power to the government which is why they are favored.

Stop justifying the actions of Congress. Stop justifying the actions of either party. Stop justifying the actions of tyrannical government in general. It is not for your safety. It is not for your wellbeing (as clearly demonstrated in this book), it is for their power and their power alone.

Stop watching the media which continues to push and/or defend the agendas of politicians who are clearly not thinking about the people of this great nation. If you are not watching, advertisers will not buy. If advertisers do not buy, the media group will close shop. It is simple.

As we saw with Gandhi, being resolved is critical. You need to keep trying, keep posting, keep referring, keep calling, and keep yelling. Never stop. You will never win unless you resolved to do so.

Always advocate, push for, and support education reform.

Let me just reiterate a couple of extremely important points. Be loud! Don't be afraid to speak up and often. Be as loud as your opponents. Be louder if you can be. Be prepared for chaos: have a plan. Be prepared with food: have a stash. Be prepared for foe: have protection. Be prepared with shelter: have a place . . . or two.

We must eliminate the IRS and the corruption it breeds— IE: Tyrannically taking money away from the people. But the nation still needs some kind of "*revenue*". This could be solved by switching to something like HR 25. It is imperative that you support this and inform your friends, neighbors and family.

We need to rid ourselves of the "*central bank*"—IE: FED RES. The entire reason this nation flourished in the times that it did was due in great part to our lack of central banks, and/or our mission to strike them down as they rose up. Think Colonial Script. Once again, this can be addressed through HR 25 and it is imperative that you support this and inform your friends, neighbors and family.

Now, understand that this is just a basic list of things that you can do to change things and things that you can do to be prepared. I do not want to hear that you cannot do anything about what is going on because obviously there is a lot you CAN do. Can you change what the federal government has done? Not right now and not by yourself. But together . . . together we can!

And finally, understand that time is not on your side. Do not procrastinate!

Becoming a *"Prepper"*

Since when did being prepared for something become a bad idea? Would planning for a retirement outside of social security make you a *"conspiracy theorist"*? So why is it somehow a bad idea to be prepared for the numerous reasons presented each and every year as far as survival goes?

Furthermore, the government appears to be extremely confused when it comes to its own policies. You have some parts of the government telling you to prepare for all kinds of disasters, but other departments calling people who do prepare *"domestic terror threats"*. That is what intellectuals refer to as a *"mixed signal"*.

The biggest misconception when it comes to being prepared is that everyone who prepares thinks that the world is coming to an end or believes that the zombie apocalypse is upon us. That is not the case at all. What preparing is all about is understanding the cycles, understanding the threats and recognizing the opportunity for things like Grid-Failure to occur. It simply means understanding that things do not last forever and it is always a good idea to be prepared for the worst case scenario. Perhaps it means listening to the FEMA announcements being broadcast on late night radio, or the numerous government agencies already warning of such disasters and telling us that we would be idiots to not be prepared.

However you want to look at this, we have to remember that during a crisis situation, those who were prepared are usually the ones who live to tell the story of how so many others suffered and died. People who are prepared generally do not think of it as preparing for the end of the world. Instead, it is ensuring the situation so that they will be around after the crisis has passed.

There are three primary ways to go about *"prepping"* for a disaster scenario. One is prepping for a shelter in place scenario, and the second is to prep for a *"bug-out"* scenario, and the third is prep for both.

"Shelter-in-place" means to take immediate shelter where you are—at home, work, school, or in between. It may also mean *"seal the room;"* in other words, take steps to prevent outside air from coming in. This is because local authorities may instruct you to *"shelter-in-place"* if chemical or radiological contaminants are released into the environment. (CDC—http://emergency.cdc.gov/ preparedness/shelter/) Perhaps you got the news a little late and you are trapped in an area where society has completely broken down. Your opportunity to bug out has passed and you need to barricade yourself in the house. Knowing how to do this and having the supplies to wait out the crisis is key, because going outside might get you killed.

"Bugging out" means to leave your immediate area. If you are bugging out, the best places to bug out to are usually locations with few human inhabitants. In other words, you would be seeking a location well outside any population

center. This of course, alludes to the idea that you might need to be well-practiced in the bushcraft or camping lifestyle. Well-practiced is the phrase used because during the crisis is not the best time to start learning how to do things required for survival. When you plan your bugout, it is best to figure out about four different locations that you could go that do not rely on the same routes to get there. This is because roads can sometimes be blocked or destroyed.

It is imperative that you make your decisions quickly and wisely in regard to bugging out or sheltering in place. Hurricanes, disease, earthquakes, floods, chemical leaks, societal breakdowns, economic collapse, terrorist attacks, or World War III—these are all possibilities in your future and making (or not making) a decision could mean life or death.

Something to keep in mind: if you are prepared and you live in a highly populated area, you are a target. The best of neighbors can easily become an enemy if they are not properly prepared but they know you are. This is also a hint to get them on board, getting their preparedness in order. The scenarios listed above should change the plan of action. For instance, if deadly disease is ravaging the area, the last thing you probably want to do is get out and expose your family to it. Shelter in place would more than likely be your best bet. On the other hand, a societal breakdown or economic collapse might be a good reason to bug out. This is where being smart and thinking ahead is vital.

The hardest concept for many to visualize is the start of such events. It will not be only you trying to survive, and it will more than likely not be like what you have seen on TV. Imagine the chaos of thousands of people attempting to evacuate the area at the same time. Imagine the thousands of people who were unprepared trying to gather resources during a crisis event. Riots and chaos can spring up in a minute, which means you need to be ready ahead of time.

While it is important to keep up on current events, we have seen time and time again that government is not to be relied upon when it comes to your safety. They will usually not be able to tell you something is wrong until it is too late because undoubtedly, they are finding out about the same time you are. If you are caught in the middle of whatever crisis may occur, they probably will not be able to get to you for a while. One need only look back at 9/11, Katrina, Sandy, etc., for evidence of this. Their number one priority is to contain the situation, not necessarily save you. Yes, this is not comforting news, but it is true.

There are many things that can kill you in a disaster scenario. However, it is safe to say that death among victims in a disaster scenario mostly occur by indecision, dehydration, starvation, the elements, and being completely unprepared for the issues they would face.

The last thing you want to do is to begin buying emergency food and water supplies once you hear the news talking about a possible threat. When the military and police start hitting the streets in mass, it is safe to say that something is going on. The best thing any prepper can do is be aware of your surroundings. Pay attention. Long lines at banks, grocery stores, gas stations, hardware stores, etc. These are signs that something serious is about to go down. Joining these lines is a dangerous proposition and one that is simply not recommended.

You need to have already made your decision and either be loading your supplies into your vehicle or buttoning up your house during this time. Mentally, I am sure you can already visualize the benefit of being prepared ahead of time. While the community is panicking, you can already be in motion.

Prepping is not something you should put off until tomorrow. As demonstrated, these events are a reality of life, and some of the more severe events seem ever more likely in the coming years. What you do now, could save the lives of yourself and your family. So think . . . and act!

There are many resources available on the internet when it comes to prepping. There is no "*correct*" way to "*prep*" short of the idea that you are addressing indecision, dehydration, starvation, and the elements. These are the big ones and the ones you should focus on. In other words, you can probably get by without a Ham radio, but you can't get by without water.

Indecision—You can help overcome indecision by being prepared to both shelter in place and bug out. This is because when you have the supplies, the question is no longer "*what do I need?*" it is simply "*which is the wiser?*" You will save yourself an incredible amount of time by simply having what you need where you need it. You will not be in some line surrounded by highly stressed out and dangerous people who though it could never happen to them.

Dehydration—Water is vital for life. It is said that a healthy sedentary adult should drink 1.5 liters of water per day. If you activity is increased due to stress or workload, this amount will increase. Water provides many vital functions in our body. It carries minerals, vitamins and glucose to our cells, it removes waste products including toxins from our organs, it transports nutrients throughout our bodies, and it regulates our body temperature, and is vital for proper brain function. Having the ability to acquire or clean water is crucial. This is number one on many lists; it should probably be number one on yours.

Starvation—Food is pretty important as well. Having food ready to eat when you need it will keep you moving and keep you thinking. Health begins to breakdown when you do not provide the body what it needs. A solid nutritional base will keep you going stronger and longer. If ready to eat food is not an option for whatever reason, having the ability to hunt for it becomes critical.

Elements—The cold and heat can kill you. If you are not prepared to warm your body or you do not have what is needed to shield yourself from the sun, you increase your potential for untimely death.

Cost—There are several different ways to look at the cost element of preparing yourself. One way to look at it is that it can be expensive and you can wait until something major occurs before you start. This is of course a really naive way to look at it because by the time these things are truly needed, they will be priceless and more than likely unavailable for purchase.

The second way to look at this would be as an investment. Understand that everything you purchase in preparedness can and more than likely will be utilized at some point. You can always drink water, you will always need food, and you will always need clothes. As far as the extra gear, you will be practicing your skills with friends and family so you're not out anything there either. It will be utilized.

"Preparing on a Budget"

Below is a list of suggested food items to store. You can store these in basic black truck boxes found for under $20 at your local big box store, or just store them in your pantry. The truck boxes tend to be a better idea because they are transported easier and they are at the ready. This is a personal choice though.

These are usually easily acquired by spending roughly $5 extra each visit to the store. Simply pick up one or two of the items listed each time you go. Remember, ANYTHING you get now will be a great help during a crisis. Be mindful of things you would actually be able to cook and be willing to eat though. If you do not like rice, you probably should not buy rice. If you do not like wheat, you should not buy wheat. If all you like is peanut butter and oats, then a mixture of salt, peanut butter, oats, and honey will be great! Just think about what you are willing to eat and go from there. This is not an overly complicated process.

Special Note: If you have a cell phone, you must understand that service may or may not be in place depending on the crisis event. That being said, it would be a good idea to have a charged phone just in case, so a mobile charger is a great recommendation.

Salt—salt is vital for life and so is iodine. Pick up iodized salt and make sure you have plenty of it. 1/8 of a teaspoon twice a day for each person.

Raw Honey—This keeps for a very long time and can be used for its antibiotic properties and wound healing.

Alcohol—Whiskey, Vodka, etc . . . —Optional but not a bad idea.

Hard Grains such as millet, spelt or wheat may not be a bad idea.

Soft grains such as quick oats are great and keep easy.

Beans such as pinto, kidney, lentils, black, and blackeyed etc., are great and can actually be used as seeds to grow more. Of course, this means bagged, not canned.

- All Purpose Flour
- Pasta
- White Rice (up to 10 years)
- Coconut oil—Coconut oil has one of the longest shelf lives of any kind of oil. It can last for over 2 years and is a great item to add to your survival food supply list.
- Canned Tuna
- Canned Meats

- Canned Vegetables & Fruits
- Peanut Butter
- Coffee
- Tea
- Ramen Noodles
- Hard Candy
- Powdered milk
- Dried herbs and spices
- Lighters
- Toilet Paper
- Soaps
- Bottled Water
- Vitamins
- Medicines
- Bandages
- Peroxide
- Lighter fluid
- Charcoal
- Duct Tape

Understand that what was given to you there was a basic budget prep list that will get you by in a shelter in place scenario. This could be considered a basic starter list for those simply trying to get SOMETHING squared away. Some of it will also work in a bugout scenario, but there are some other items you will need. Now we are going to get into a more comprehensive list of things that you may want to consider acquiring when you can. The list is comprised of numerous lists from across the prepping community. You will find lists with more, some with less, if you search *"prepper lists"* or *"bug out lists"*. Remember, these are just suggestions and things to consider while you prepare. Only YOU will know what is best for you situation.

The number one thing I stress here is that in a crisis situation, you may be stuck in a *"without rule of law"* situation. You must prepare yourself accordingly.

- A quality pack—(ILBE, back pack, ALICE Pack, etc.)
- A quality knife (Survival Knife)
- Sawyer All In One Water Filter
- A Bandana
- Energy / Protein bars—a few days' worth.
- Multi-tool, quality construction
- Portable capability to pre-filter / purify / disinfect water for additional 30 days or more
- Firearms
- Ammunition—no less than 500 rounds for every firearm
- Spare mags and clips
- Cleaning tools for all firearms
- Solar Powered or Crank Light
- 100 ft 550lb Parachord
- Sewing Kit
- First Aid Kit
- Maps of surrounding area
- Three to seven complete changes of rugged clothes for all members
- Three complete changes of sleep clothes for all members

- Seven changes of underclothes for each member
- One or two pair of rugged, waterproof boots for each member
- One pair of comfortable shoes (sneakers, sandals, etc.) for each member
- Several Outer gear sets (boots, gloves, mittens, scarves, hats, etc.) for all climates (cold weather, rain, etc.)
- Quantity of various materials for repairs and creation of clothing
- Hand held radio (FRS, GMRS, Ham, CB, etc.), transmit and receive, with extra batteries or solar charger
- CB Radio
- Crank powered AM/FM radio.
- List of Contacts
- List frequencies
- Security system that monitors home perimeter
- Fire extinguishers
- Add laminate to exterior windows (resists break-ins, etc.)
- Pay one month of bills with cash on hand
- Supply of hard currency (silver, gold, etc.)
- Supply of barter goods
- Block Sun UV rays
- Insect Repellent
- 30 days of life saving prescription medications
- 30 days of OTC and "*maintenance*" medications
- Dental Hygiene Tools—Tooth Brush / Toothpaste
- Flatware—spoons, knives, forks, etc.
- Stored food for 30 days

- Stored water for 90 days or more
- Portable capability for minimum-prepared foods for 14 days
- Tools for gathering more food (hunt, fish, trap/snare, gather wild plants, etc.)
- Cookware that can be used over an open fire (pots, pans, kettles, etc.)
- Equipment to cook over fire pit (grates, tripods, hooks, etc.)
- Forms of entertainment (games, books, pens, paper, cards, football, frisbee, baseball/throwing ball, soccer ball, etc.)
- N100 or P100 masks/filters
- Nitrile gloves
- Contact Cleaner/Holder
- Two pairs of eyeglasses, both with current prescription
- Eyeglass repair kit
- Eyeglass retaining straps
- Denture care
- Floss
- Nail trimmers
- Comb/brush hair
- Razors
- Deodorant/antiperspirant
- Lotions
- Tweezers
- Cotton Swabs
- Feminine hygiene items
- Compost garbage and waste

- Spare buckets
- Lots of plastic trash bags
- Pet care needs, special medications, food, toys, etc., for 90+ days
- Tent(s)/Tarps, enough space to contain all members and gear
- Sleeping bag or other bedding (for sub-freezing temperatures)
- Ability to make fire in, at least, 3 different ways
- Spare sheets and blankets
- Pillows (as needed)
- Alternate heating source for home
- Shelter repair supplies: plywood, wood strips, plastic sheeting, screws, nails, etc.
- Tools—Basic screwdriver set, Hammer, Supply of nails, screws, parts & tools to repair critical plumbing items
- Heavy Tools—Shovel, ax, saw, etc.
- Twine, Rope and wire
- Scissors (need several pair for different tasks; a good set of scissors is indispensable)
- 'Fix a flat' or Slime
- Self-vulcanizing plug kit and/or a bottle of Yarrow
- Air compressor (12 VDC)
- Hose clamps, various sizes (or hose wrap or duct tape)
- Siphon hose
- Funnels (keep in mind that a funnel for your fuel tank will probably be different from the ones that you use under the hood)
- Full-sized spare tire

- Maps already stored in vehicle
- Basic spare parts (hoses, belts, sparks plugs, fasteners, etc.)
- Extra fluids (oil, coolant, transmission fluid, washer fluid, etc.)
- Tool kit, stored in vehicle
- Jumper cables
- Recovery strap/tow rope
- Ability to gather large quantities of water for cleaning (rain, etc.)
- Dedicated "*dirty water*" containers (waste)
- NOAA weather radio
- Store a couple of 5 gallon gas cans (full of course) in your garage or shed. This will eliminate your need to wait in line at the gas station.
- And if you have the money-Generator, with enough capacity to power critical needs for 14+ days and enough fuel to power it. There are solar options which are good to consider for this.

The idea is to work yourself up to about one year's worth of food, in any combination of everyday, minimum-prepared, and long-term storage foods, with the experience and equipment to prepare it. It is also recommended that you have a portable capability of minimum-prepared foods for 30 days or more (for traveling). What I personally recommend is to detail out what you eat and just start buying extra. It does not have to be some huge bank busting endeavor.

In closing, remember to keep your plans and your supplies quiet. Once again, if you tell everyone about what you have, then they will know where to go if things get bad. You become a target because you have told everyone that you are. Teach your children not to talk about your preparedness plans, equipment or supplies as well and always keep your important documents in a fire- resistant safe.

It would also be a good idea to have a defense plan for your entire property, an inventory list for quick reference and a written plan for what your actions will be for all conceivable events. These become more solid when you write them down and they are more easily refined when conceptualized on paper. This will also help you in determining what plans need to be activated by the specific event criteria such as disease, terrorist attack, etc.

I hope this helps. Once again, the above lists are suggestions as found throughout the internet. There are much more comprehensive lists and ideas for both sheltering in place and for bugging out. Some people prefer much less and what they refer to as the bare essentials. That is fine, too.

The biggest key is getting started doing something. Even if you were only able to secure another week's worth of food, you have just given yourself another week's worth of opportunity to survive.

The biggest tip on this stuff is to not stress out about this process. One step at a time will get you what you need. Seriously! One step at a time.

A Better Party

Historically speaking, there have been a lot of political parties in this great nation. This is kind of sad really because George Washington warned us that having a party system would tear us apart. Sure, he accepted the idea that people want to organize and operate within groups like political parties, but he argued that every government has recognized political parties as an enemy and has sought to repress them because of their tendency to seek more power than other groups and take revenge on political opponents. Can you imagine?

As addressed in early in this book, today we see the constants created by the powerful party system. The government has increased in power and policies have been handed down from one administration to the next. We have seen a continual decline in our personal liberties. The destruction of our economy seems almost complete. Literally, both of the most powerful parties are to blame.

Look at what we have today. Both parties literally work hand in hand in seeking more power and taking revenge on EVERY opponent, including their own constituents. Surely, Americans could figure out a better way, right? Are we really stuck with the Republicans and Democrats forever? Is this government going to just grow and grow like the cancer it already is, until it consumes the body and destroys it?

Understand that I am with Washington on this one. Still, I understand and respect the idea of the party scheme. The current party system is severely flawed though and it needs fixed. I think most could probably agree with that. So, if we are forced to play the party game, can we not improve on it based out of what we already know? Let us pretend for a second that I could change this whole thing and introduce a party that would somehow be better than the "*options*" we already have. What might that look like?

First of all, I would create a party whose sole mission was to defend the rights of the individual. This probably goes without saying. What if the party supported the people's right to exercise sole dominion over their own lives, and supported people having the right to live in whatever manner they choose, so long as they do not forcibly interfere with the equal right of others to live in whatever manner they choose?

What if this party would deny the right of any government to violate the rights of any individual: namely, the right to life, the right to liberty of speech and action, and the right to property that cannot be taken away via confiscation, nationalization, and eminent domain, etc.?

What if the party insisted that a government could not violate individual rights, or interfere in areas such as voluntary and contractual relations among individuals?

What if one of the general premises of this new party was to encourage people to make decisions for themselves, and to accept responsibility for the consequences of the choices they make. No individual, group, or government could initiate force against any other individual, group, or government.

A party that would encourage an individual's engagement or abstinence in any religious activities that do not violate the rights of others?

What if we created this party to support the Bill of Rights 100%? We would not have to worry about government agencies spying on the people or targeting citizens just because they like a certain candidate! Or better yet, creating a party that would repeal all laws creating "*crimes*" without victims. We might actually cease to be the nation who incarcerates the most people in the world.

For the sake of equality, this party would ensure that the government does not have the authority to define, license or restrict personal relationships, because consenting adults should be free to choose their own sexual practices and personal relationships as long as they do not infringe in the rights of another.

Of course it would have to oppose the prosecution of individuals for exercising their rights of self-defense or any laws at any level of government requiring registration of, or restricting, the ownership, manufacture, or transfer or sale of firearms or ammunition.

And what if this party ensured that the proper role of government in the economic realm was to protect property rights, adjudicate disputes, and provide a legal framework in which voluntary trade was protected? Plus, no redistribution programs!

We could support a clean and healthy environment and sensible use of our natural resources, and oppose all government control of energy pricing, allocation, and production.

I imagine a country where everyone is entitled to keep the fruits of their labor. This party could call for the repeal of the income tax, the abolishment of the Internal Revenue Service and all federal programs and services not required under the US Constitution.

The party could favor free-market banking, with unrestricted competition among banks and depository institutions of all types. Heck, you do the same with health insurance while we were at it, and allow people to purchase health insurance across state lines.

And just to keep everyone honest, this party would support the idea that whenever any form of government becomes destructive of individual liberty, it is the right of the people to alter or to abolish it, and to agree to such new governance as to them shall seem most likely to protect their liberty.

It sure sounds nice. Of course, you are probably saying to yourself something to the effect of *"Nice dream, could never happen!"* or *"No one would allow such a party to even exist."* Well, you are right. It is a nice dream, because one could imagine that most people in this great nation would probably subscribe to just about all these ideas. That is of course if they love the Constitution.

My bigger question is why is this so farfetched? If you believe that having a party like this is a pipe dream, why even care? Have you really given up on your principles?

Here is the deal my friends, this party already exists and is actually gaining strength by the day because more and more people are figuring out that this is exactly what this country needs. This party is exactly why some in Washington are seen as trouble makers.

What you have just read is actually a decent portion of the party platform of the Libertarian Party. Are you shocked? I know I was when I first read their platform. Does that platform sound more like how it was supposed to be?

Look, the whole point is this chapter was simply to get you to read something you have probably bypassed a hundred times because you thought you knew about it. I know, because I did it too and I was lucky enough to have someone slide me some info.

Take some time to look them up. If you have to be a part of a party, you might as well be a part of the party that actually represents your positions. Imagine if everyone actually joined the party that REALLY fit their positions. I would imagine the Libertarian party would be first.

Remember, the lesser of two evils is still evil, and if we are going down anyway, you might as well make a stand on your principles while you can. What else do you have to lose at this point?

Can You Question With Boldness?

It has been said that only those with something to hide would oppose certain lines of questioning. In fact, that argument has been made AGAINST Americans who fear Constitutional infringements when it comes to privacy laws, voter ID's, universal background checks on firearms and so on.

As a nation and as a culture, we are highly inquisitive. Even our founder Thomas Jefferson suggested that we question everything with boldness. Today, we question our neighbors actions, the actions of others states, and even our own family and friends. People in general are highly skeptical about everything these days. In fact, you could state something having every single fact necessary to prove the point, and people still need to go figure it out for themselves before believing it.

The government is no exception and they often foster this behavior. The government encourages the questioning of your neighbors with programs such as "*See something, say something*", or the Neighborhood Watch Program, where they have encouraged bridge workers, shopping retailers, hoteliers, garbage collectors, patrol officers and your next-door neighbors to notify authorities if they witness something "out of the ordinary".

Everyone is supposed to question ever y thing and everyone . . . with one tiny exception. You are not supposed to question the motives or actions of the government. So are we led to believe that perhaps it is because the government has something to hide? Surely not! The government is our friend, and would never hurt us . . . right?

To believe the government would do something to hurt the people on purpose is preposterous and to suggest such a thing is considered conspiratorial and a clear sign of a domestic terror threat; at least that is what the government and mainstream media is telling you. "There is nothing to see here folks!" Usually there is something to see. Oddly enough, millions follow this advice and the advice provided by the state run media, which is to blindly follow anything and everything that is fed to you by the Feds and the media and to react emotionally instead of intellectually to the questions that may come up countering the official position.

Let me help you break this down into a logical processes that is easy to digest. A "*conspiracy theory*" is nothing more than a belief that a covert but influential organization is responsible for a circumstance or event. A conspiracy in of itself is simply a secret plan by a group to do something unlawful or harmful. So to state this another way, a conspiracy theorist is simply someone who thinks a cover group did something harmful and unlawful.

On March 13, 1962, a document was drafted by the Joint Chiefs of Staff, and sent to the Secretary of Defense. It was called "*Justification for US Military Intervention in Cuba (TS)*". Some might know this as the Northwoods Memorandum or simply "*Operation Northwoods*" (DOD, Memorandum for the Secretary of Defense, 1962).

What this document suggested was that the CIA, (a covert but influential organization) should commit false acts of terrorism against Americans. Essentially, the CIA would commit unlawful and harmful acts including hijackings and bombings in the United States against Americans in an effort to " . . . *place the United States in the apparent position of suffering defensible grievances from a rash and irresponsible government of Cuba and to develop an international image of a Cuban threat to peace in the Western Hemisphere.*" In other words, these acts of domestic terrorism were to be blamed on Cuba in order to bolster support for a war against them.

Thankfully, President Kennedy rejected the proposals.

What should we call this? National Security? Seriously, what do you call a covert military or paramilitary operation designed to deceive in such a way that the operations appear as though they are being carried out by other entities, groups or nations than those who actually planned and executed them?

The term you seek is *"False Flag"*. That is the official position. The people who figured it out are conspiracy theorists. The part that you have to come to grips with is the fact that the conspiracy theorists were right!

The government plans to commit unlawful and harmful acts under the flag of the Communist Cubans in an effort to gain support for going to war against them. Not only is this conspiracy, but proof of the desire to commit false flags against the American people, carried out by the very government tasked with protecting them.

Right off the bat, there are going to be those who will justify the actions or say that it was an isolated incident, like being abused by your spouse. Well, that is great that you want so bad to believe that such things could not or would not occur again (or have before), but what is it that they say about dealing with domestic violence? Oh yeah, *"If it has happened once, it will happen again."* If violence or even the threat of violence has happened more than once, it is extremely likely to happen again. The violence usually gets worse over time, increasing in both frequency and severity. Is what we talk about here any different? Are you going to justify the abusive partner here too?

What exactly is wrong with asking questions about such events? If there is evidence to suggest the official story is false, would it not be wise to question with boldness that story? If there is nothing to hide, why does the government withhold the answers or dodge the questions entirely? National Security? That is what they keep telling us and yet, these situations continue.

-   Conspiracy Theorists ask questions and are considered a threat for doing so.
-   This means that they are considered a threat for having asked certain questions.
-   Now ask yourself, *"Why is someone who asked certain questions, such a threat exactly?"*

Government officials lead you to believe that questions are only a threat when the person being asked the questions has something to hide. This plays in their favor when they are asking you questions and digging for information. It does not seem to work both ways however because if you are asking the questions and the answer to such questions are an actual threat the operations being undertaken by those who were asked, you are a "*Conspiracy Theorist*". Ironic is it not?

You do realize of course, that according to Occam's Razor, the government is hiding a lot!

What are they hiding exactly? That is a great question and one not easily answered. Regardless, those questions are irrelevant unless you are in a position to accept the answers you could possibly find. This is an important caveat to this equation as we know that most people in this great nation simply could not handle the repercussions of such answers.

The best advice I can give when you are seeking answers, is truly and literally to ask questions. You need to be that little kid who repeatedly asks "*why*". That is the only way you will find the answers you seek. When it comes to "*conspiracy theory*", the idea is to boil it down and follow the Three Rule Method.

Let us use the Conspiracy Theory of "*chemtrails*" as an example. Many classify this as a conspiracy theory for whatever reason. However, did you know that "*chemtrails*" are real?

The chemtrail conspiracy theory posits that SOME trails left by aircraft are chemical or biological agents deliberately sprayed at high altitudes for purposes undisclosed to the general public and directed by various government officials.

To find whether or not this is true, it is a good idea to use the Three Rule Method. In order to effectively do that though, you must take the greater position and break it down into pieces like so:

Are any aircraft spraying things at high altitudes?

Yes! There is something call "*geoengineering*" or simply "*weather modification*" in which aircraft ranging in size from small prop planes to the large Boeing 747, attempt to engage in something known as "*Cloud Seeding*".

This is a process which seeks to bring rain to parched farmland by dispersing particles of silver iodide or solid carbon dioxide into rain-bearing clouds (Britannica, 2013).

Can the trails behind some aircraft be chemical or biological?

Yes! As we just discovered, we know they are spraying Silver Iodide. Silver Iodide is classified as a chemical and even has its own Chemical Codes (PANNA, 2010).

Is this effort directed by various government officials?

Yes! Not only are the larger aircraft used government contracted, (such as Evergreen Aviation) but the research aspect alone has government written all over it (Evergreen, 2013).

In fact, according to several sources, even the CIA helped fund a study by the National Academy of Sciences (NAS) that investigates whether humans could use geoengineering to stop climate change (Williams R., 2013). However, this is not just a government directive. Universities across this nation are involved in it as well and so are other nations around the globe.

Are these operations being disclosed to the public?

That depends on what you mean by "*disclosed*". How many people in your neighborhood have heard of this?

This is not a "*conspiracy theory*" at all. In fact, it is a very obvious fact. Yet, the government wishes to remain quiet about these activities. Sure, you can find the information but it is not exactly being delivered to your door step. Why?

The easiest way to find this answer is to ask what is being sprayed. So, let us ask this basic question. What exactly is being sprayed out of the large aircraft leaving trails of chemicals in the sky?

We already know it is chemicals such as silver iodide, but what is silver Iodide? According to the chemical charts you can find all over the internet and in the chemistry books in your school, etc., you will find that silver iodide acts as fungicide, an herbicide, and a microbiocide (PANNA, 2010). That does not sound too bad until you think about this falling on your crops.

If you have weeds, what do you buy at the store? A herbicide right? A herbicide is a substance that is toxic to plants and is used to destroy unwanted vegetation. So what happens when you put this in clouds and it rains down on the crops? Does it have the potential to kill them? Perhaps. What about your health or that of your kids who are opening their mouth and catching the rain? Does that sound like a good idea? Do you think people might get upset? How do you think this might play into other "*conspiracie*s", such as with companies like Monsanto?

Do you think the people as a whole might get upset at the idea that the government is spraying poison on their crops, lawns, etc.? Probably. So is this really a conspiracy theory? Sure it is . . . but it does not make it any less true!

Think about it, there is a group committing harmful and potentially unlawful acts against your property and your body for that matter. What would happen if you fed poison to someone else and they were not aware? Would a crime have been committed?

The funny part is that we could do this all day and still not even scratch the surface of all the things that you have probably been misled on.

So why is everyone so quick to call someone a conspiracy theorist (as though that were a bad thing) when that person sees a flaw in an official story? It is rather simple. These people are scared to death of what the truth would mean. So far, in this chapter, we have covered two "*conspiracy theories*" that are very real and I can imagine many are scared to death to cover much more.

Do not worry. I am not going to break down each and every event. I would suggest however that you be willing to explore the idea that perhaps the official stories that are provided are nothing more than a story to keep you pacified. And if you seek the truth, you need to ask some uncomfortable questions and utilize the Three Rule Method.

I do want to provide you some questions to research though. There are plenty of questions to ask in each of these instances but a few questions will more than suffice. Before I provide these questions though, I want you to reflect on an article written by David K Shipler in The New York Times on April 28, 2012. I will provide you the first couple paragraphs because I feel it really drives home the point of this chapter:

> The United States has been narrowly saved from lethal terrorist plots in recent years—or so it has seemed. A would-be suicide bomber was intercepted on his way to the Capitol; a scheme to bomb synagogues and shoot Stinger missiles at military aircraft was developed by men in Newburgh, N.Y.; and a fanciful idea to fly explosive-laden model planes into the Pentagon and the Capitol was hatched in Massachusetts.

> But all these dramas were facilitated by the F.B.I., whose undercover agents and informers posed as terrorists offering a dummy missile, fake C-4 explosives, a disarmed suicide vest and rudimentary training. Suspects naïvely played their parts until they were arrested.

The point? That you are constantly being deceived. The people were sold these stories as victories in this war against terrorism. In response, the people have furthered their support when it has turned out that perhaps the only threat we faced was that of our own government. Act accordingly.

So, here are some basic questions:

Pearl Harbor:

- What was the significance of Lieutenant Commander Arthur McCollum's memo dated October 7, 1940, and what was Roosevelt's reaction?
- What did Joseph C. Grew (the US ambassador to Japan) do on January 27, 1941?
- What did Roosevelt do in the summer of 1941, (knowing the above information ahead of time) that prompted the attack?

Gulf of Tonkin:

- What did the US Navy fail to hit on August 4, 1964?
- What happened as a result of the incident?

9/11:

- Why have over 2,000 architects and engineers, come out to say that the World Trade Center Building 7 was brought down by controlled demolition on 9/11?
- In the history of the world, how many skyscrapers have completely collapse due to fire, plane crashes or bombings?
- What is "*NORAD EXERCISES Hijack Summary*" or "*Vigilant Guardian*"?

- The Patriot Act was signed into law as a result of the attacks 45 days after the fact, but when was it written?

Sandy Hook:

- Why did an off Duty SWAT Officer who was armed with a gun, run off into the woods instead of helping the students? Why was he apprehended by responding officers?
- Why did Senate Minority Leader John McKinney want pictures and special exemptions in the state Freedom of Information Act for families who lost members in the Sandy Hook Elementary School massacre and why were contractors involved in the demolition of the Sandy Hook Elementary School, being required to sign confidentiality agreements that prohibit them from publicly discussing the site, taking photographs or disclosing information about the school?
- What is the connection to the Libor Scandal?
- Was there a government drill in the area?

Aurora, Colorado

- Why were there reports of a second shooter, and why were there two sets of the gear, but only one arrest?
- What is the connection to the Libor Scandal?
- Wasn't there a government drill going on in the area here as well?

Operation Fast and Furious:

- What is Operation Fast and Furious and what is gunwalking?
- Who is ultimately responsible?
- Is anyone in trouble?

Boston Bombing:

- Is it weird to anyone else that the officers from Sandy Hook looked just like the officers in Boston?
- How come the backpack that was found was different than the backpack worn by the suspects?
- So what exactly was "*Operation Urban Shield*" and why is that significant?
- Am I the only one who notices that there is always a government drill in the area of these horrible events?

Here are some other random questions:

- What is the Libor Scandal?
- What is Agenda 21?
- What is a "*crisis actor*"?
- What do Dyess Air Force base in South Carolina, Lindsey Graham's threat that a nuclear strike in that region was possible, and Navy Vice Adm. Tim Giardina, all have in common?

- As you know, many of the people involved in recent shootings were under psychiatric care and on psychotropic drugs. So why are guns to blame?
- What is H.A.A.R.P.?
- What do Maj. Gen. Ralph Baker, Gen. William "*Kip*" Ward, Rear Admiral Charles Gaouette and General Carter Ham all have in common?
- For that matter, why have over 190 high ranking military officers, including many senior commanding generals, been demoted or relieved of duty since 2008?

Are these questions offensive? What can possibly come about by asking question like the ones we have asked here today? Maybe you will come up with the same answers the media has provided. Or maybe, you come to your own conclusions and your own theories instead of relying on someone else to do it for you.

This is it. There is no such thing as a dumb question! If someone seeks knowledge or questions an official story, they are right to do so having been provided more than enough evidence to suggest that such questions are in their better interests. Progress has never been made in any facet of life without the benefit of a question beforehand.

During the time of the founders, many believed that thunder and lightning were the wrath of God. I wonder if Benjamin Franklin was considered a conspiracy theorist for questioning the official position, or a hero for discovering electricity. The truth was ultimately better than the ignorance that literally kept everyone in the dark. You should think about that.

The point is that asking questions is never a bad thing. If someone chooses to label you a conspiracy theorist for asking questions, then they have effectively demonstrated their ability to blindly follow and given ample reason for you to distance yourself from them. They are an ignorant poison to your mind. These are the people who would jump off a bridge when told to do so. Your parents warned you against people like this and it would be wise to listen.

In Closing

We have covered a lot in this book and undoubtedly there is much you are now concerned about in regard to the state of our union. I would like to offer a different perspective though.

Personally, I do not view it all as doom and gloom. Just like every other cycle to come around, there will be something worth living for and working for. Just like every other dictatorship or tough time, there will be life afterwards and an opportunity to make life better than it was before.

Understand though, I am not saying it will be easy. The coming years will undoubtedly be some of the toughest times Americans have ever had to face. I have said it before and I will say it a hundred more times: "*The time in which we currently live, will be studied and pondered for hundreds, if not thousands of years!*"

That also means that everyone has an opportunity to help make this right. Everyone is a player in the grand scheme of things. Whatever happens from here will literally be whatever we make of it. Are we going to remain silent while we crumble to a globalist or social agenda, or are we going to get loud and defend our way of life and what we know is right? Are we going to fail ourselves or are we going to stand up and defend the Constitution?

The true radicals are taking over because so many are afraid to even say anything. It is like listening to someone talking in a theater, so many are afraid to tell that person to shut up because they would rather avoid confrontation.

We need to find that resolve. If you do, our Constitution may just have a chance. You have to know your principles and be willing to stand on them. If you do, our Constitution may just have a chance. You have to be willing to see the world for what it is and see your place in it.

Patriotism is not a little flag pin you wear on your coat. It is the reason you wear the little flag pin on your coat. Patriotism is an enormous love of this country and the willingness to defend it at all costs, no matter what that price may be. If there is a term that hinders this love and devotion more than the term "*politically correct*" that would be extremely surprising.

We live in a nation now where someone who waves the American flag outside of their own home can be fined and at the same time thousands of criminal immigrants can storm the streets with Mexican flags while turning the American flag upside-down and they are called brave. We have allowed this.

During his campaign, Mr. Barack Hussein Obama said he no longer wears an American flag lapel pin because it has become a substitute for "*true patriotism*" since the Sept. 11, 2001, terrorist attacks. Perhaps this is true, but pretending to love a country while at the same time trying to turn it into some sort of socialized state is not exactly patriotism either.

I agree that Patriotism is much more than flying a flag. It means defending the principles of this republic. It is defending your fellow American. It is defending our borders. It is defending our way of life. It is making sure that the tomorrow we leave for our children is better than what we were given. It is making sure our children grow up in a free nation where they can achieve everything they work for.

Patriotism does not have a color, a religion, or a sexual preference either. You can be a black, gay, atheist, who believes in abortion and still be a patriot. Those who do not agree with that are ignorant because none of the descriptive words used have anything to do with loving or defending your country.

This country is great because it is so diverse. You get something new every day if you just open your eyes and talk to someone that you did not know yesterday. Can you imagine how boring this country would be if everyone was cookie cut out of themselves? There is so much we can learn from each other if most of us would just stop for a second and listen.

Without diversity, we are simple and predictable. The Constitution tells us that all men are created equal. It does not say anything about all men are created different. Most religions tell us to celebrate our differences. In the United States of America, we have the best, the brightest and the most talented individuals in the world. Numerous Olympics, innovations, and battles have shown us this and the people have come from every walk of life from the rich to the poor and from every single color and creed.

We are united in the Constitution and we will fight to the death to preserve it. That is true patriotism. This non-sense of "*God bless the country we are trying to create*" is nothing more than socialist propaganda because we already have a great nation. We already have the best foundation we could have ever asked for and the only reason it has been messed up in the past is because the PEOPLE of the United States STOPPED caring what their politicians were doing so the POLITICIANS STOPPED listening to the people! We need to get back to the Constitution instead of trying to change everything into a government-run society.

Understand that regardless of the outcome, the principles of the Constitution will carry on if you choose to carry them. The US may not end up looking like it does today, but if you want it bad enough, and we all fight hard enough, we can preserve it.

A Quick Rant about *"Free"*

I wanted to take a few minutes and vent about something that I feel encompasses many of the points within this book. When did this nation become a nation of mooches? Why are we so eager to jump on the *"Free"* bandwagon anytime someone says it? For instance, a company provides flu vaccines and people line up without even researching what they are about to inject in their bodies. This is lunacy!

Perhaps it boils down to greed. Maybe the idea of *"keeping up with the Jones'"* has really taken its toll on the American public. Perhaps *"free"* is so important because so many Americans simply do not have a lot of money anymore. The irony is however, that by subscribing to the idea of *"free"*, everyone is unknowingly making their situation even more difficult.

It seems that most people these days want everything for nothing. It is all about more money, more toys and less work if we have to work at all. Children no longer want to grow up to do something great and be famous for it; they simply want to grow up to be famous, and having certain jobs is somehow beneath them.

Few are considering or teaching the errors of these ideas. Instead, they have created television shows that exploit this and exacerbate the problem, while the American public gladly watches it. Not only do they watch it, but they follow these people as though they actually mean something. They buy their magazines, their products, and their sales pitch. Kim Kardashian is a great example of this. Sure, she is kind of pretty but who cares? Does anyone have a good reason why she is famous? Meanwhile, do you have any idea who Moses Cardenas or who Shannon Kay is?

The point is that our priorities as a nation have become distorted to say the least and this is a big reason why we are in the boat we find ourselves in. As demonstrated in previous chapters, we are following the path of other Republics accordingly. Ignore it if you want, but the problem remains.

The idea of something for nothing (or for very little) seems as though it is some kind of standard in the United States. Criminal immigrants come here to exploit that very idea. Free healthcare, free education, free monetary benefits. It is beyond that though. Our citizens are constantly finding ways to exploit the benefit programs. What is even worse is that if one does not qualify for a benefit, and cannot figure out another way to go about getting it, then they resort to frivolous lawsuits.

In February 1992, Stella Liebeck ordered a cup of coffee at the drive thru at a local McDonalds. Keeping in mind that car was not in motion; Liebeck was adding sugar to her coffee. While removing the cup's lid, Liebeck spilled her hot coffee, burning her legs. It was determined that Liebeck suffered third degree burns on over six percent of her body. Originally, Liebeck wanted $20,000 in damages. McDonalds refused to settle out of court but they should have. Liebeck was finally awarded $200,000 in compensatory damages, which was reduced to $160,000 because she was found to be twenty percent at fault. She was also awarded $2.7 million in punitive damages. Soon after, McDonalds was forced to label everything in an effort to avoid further situations of people burning themselves because too many people are stupid.

She ordered it, she paid for it (so she gained ownership) she opened it, it is common knowledge that hot coffee is hot, and she spilled it. Aside from handing someone a boiling cup of joe, how is McDonalds at fault and why should they have paid? Many people laugh about things like this but the truth is that everyone else has to pay for it. Do you think McDonalds paid for it out of their pocket? Sure, it might have only added a nickel of extra cost to your bag, but the public is who really paid for it. Of course, the public also paid the fines that this particular McDonalds had received by health inspectors during the week prior, but I digress.

Frivolous lawsuits are extremely common in America today. Everyone is trying to get something for nothing. In 1996, a physical therapist in Florida named Paul Shimkonis sued a strip club claiming he got whiplash from a lap dancer's large breasts smacking him in the face. Shimkonis said he felt that he suffered physical harm and mental anguish from the large breasts. He went on to say that the breasts felt like "*cement blocks*" hitting him. So Shimkonis tried to sue the bar for $15,000. Although it was denied, the point is that this is yet another example of people just trying to get something for nothing.

These may be dated examples and there were literally hundreds to choose from, however the point is that the idea of something for nothing has poisoned our society in ways that are almost impossible to reverse at this point. The fear is that the cause and effect scenarios of such ideas have in fact, already begun to play themselves out.

This is one of the many reasons why healthcare costs remain so high. Medical malpractice insurance covers doctors and other professionals in the medical field for liability claims arising from their treatment of patients. Some estimates show that malpractice insurance costs anywhere in-between $42,000 to $129,000 per year or even higher. These prices are steadily increasing due in great part to frivolous lawsuits. Once again, it is the people (you and me) who end up paying the costs.

It works like this. A doctor or a doctor's office has a "*service*" they provide. They have expenses to pay as well, just like any other business. These expenses need to be recouped and are added into the price of their services. So as the price of their services increase, the price that a patient's insurance has to pay goes up. So if the insurance company has to pay more, the amount the patient has to pay increases as well.

Frivolous lawsuits and malpractice lawsuits are affecting more than just the price of healthcare; it is affecting the way doctors are doing their jobs. More than 40 percent of doctors reported avoiding prescribing proper medication because they knew the drug might be mixed up in legal action. A good example of this would be Aspirin. Even though for a good number people, Aspirin is helpful (having such results as lowering cholesterol, reducing fevers, ridding someone of their headaches etc.,) companies like Bayer are still facing lawsuits from people who had side effects using the drug. In fact, in 2001 Bayer was facing more than 8,000 lawsuits in which 6,000 of those lawsuits were being filed by people who did not even experience any side effects. According to a Towers Perrin study, the US tort liability system cost each US citizen $721 in 2001 ($205 billion total).

It is because people want something for nothing and these lawyers who are prompting these class action lawsuits and other frivolous lawsuits are reaping massive benefits as well. Personal injury lawyers walk away with 30-50 percent of any jury award to the plaintiff, plus an additional percentage of the award to cover expenses. Of course your healthcare is going through the roof. An estimated $50 billion per year is spent on unnecessary test procedures designed only to guard doctors and hospitals against malpractice claims and almost half of the money spent by physician insurers goes towards defending cases that ultimately are closed without compensation paid to the claimant. It is ridiculous.

Yes, we could discuss the lack of competition between insurers or the inability to sell health insurance across state lines as a massive culprit to the price of healthcare, but that is a different topic altogether. For that matter, we could probably discuss the doctors and medical groups that charge the social programs unbelievable amounts for the tiniest things. The point here is that when someone receives something for "*free*", someone else has to pay for it because there is always a cost to goods or services used. Who gets charged for exploiting these social programs? The American Tax Payer ultimately.

Honestly, we could discuss retail or any other industry as well. When there is an opportunity to exploit and acquire the good or service for free, or when someone figures out a way to force that industry to pay them above and beyond the service or good, the costs are passed on to the other customers.

Take the Affordable Care Act for instance. Did you really think that YOU would not be the one to pay for it? People have been warning of the repercussions of the "*Universal Healthcare*" for years. Higher taxes, higher deductibles, and canceled policies are just the beginning. Your benefits and services provided by "*free*" healthcare will eventually be reduced because the cost will simply outweigh what can truly be offered. This is not speculation; this is a recognized cause and effect scenario coming with a ridiculous amount of evidence from other nations who have attempted similar programs.

The Europeans and Canadians are now forced to reduce much of what they used to offer simply because of the rise in healthcare costs and system abuses. A 1996 front-page story in the New York Times detailed the European cutbacks. According to the article, Britain, France and Germany were all being forced to limit access to care. Rationing, already extensive, is increasing even to this day.

So what do the cutbacks really get you? Over time they get you lowered standards. In October of 2007 a startling report was released that showed what a "*universal*" type healthcare could result in. Appalling standards of care and an enormous list of failures contributed to the deaths of 331 patients in the worst outbreak of a hospital "*superbug*" ever recorded in the British National Health Service.

Due to crowded wards and a shortage of nurses as well as numerous financial problems, 1,176 people contracted Clostridium difficile over two and half years at three hospitals in Kent, a county in southeast England.

How could all of that really be to blame? Well, the Health Secretary, Alan Johnson described the failures that led to this outbreak by saying nurses were so rushed they did not have time to wash their hand and though the "*superbug*" was widespread in the wards, managers failed to act. Isolation units were not set up, and patients were left in soiled beds. Furthermore, bedpans were not decontaminated properly and in general linens were not cleaned as well as they should have been.

If there will be no office visit bill to pay, people will be able to run to the doctor every time they stub their toe or get a sniffle. Perhaps the elderly person will increase their visits as well—mostly because they are lonely and it gives them someone to talk to.

Some might think this is a good thing because no one would have to let any medical problem at all go unattended. In discussing this situation with many people that use the Canadian socialized medicine system, at this initial level of the system—it is a good thing. In Canada (not as much as some of the other countries and depending on the province), people are generally able to get in right away for any of these type of appointments.

The problems generally occur when the doctor discovers what he believes might be a more urgent problem, say suspecting lung cancer or something similar. The waiting list to get in for diagnosis testing such as MRI's or other more high level procedures is long. Some specific cancer tests are run at the rate of only one per month—that is what is available to the entire population. One screening per month even if there are 250,000 suspected cases!

That means that if you needed to be screened and diagnosed for that certain type of cancer, you could be waiting for years to get the screening appointment. Then there are the follow-up appointments with the oncologist once you have a positive result. Needless to say, by the time you actually get to the point that you have a solid diagnosis and could begin treatment—you are probably dead or at the very least unable to be saved. This keeps their numbers looking good—if someone dies but has never been actually diagnosed with lung cancer—they do not have to count it as a failure for their health system.

It does not matter how much money you have if you are on the socialized health care system. It is illegal to buy services outside of the system (in Canada at least). The Canadian officials have been known to send Canadian mothers in distress to hospitals in the United States for treatment occasionally among a few other patients as well, but these practices are few and far between. For the most part there is no way out or no way around it. Essentially, your options become limited because your options are reduced and/or governed by another.

There are similar reports from various socialist health care systems around the world such as people having to pull their own teeth because getting a dentist appointment can easily take a year or more. In some countries, because of the abuse of free doctor appointments at the lowest levels of the system, you have to wait for weeks or months to be able to be seen for even the smallest medical concern.

Now imagine the DMV. Do we have faith that the American government could handle the challenge any better than the Canadians, Australians or the Europeans when push comes to shove? What makes anyone really believe that our government will do a good job with healthcare?

The point is that nothing is free and that perhaps the cost of free is much more expensive than the alternative. There is always going to be catch somewhere and to think otherwise is naïve. If you are one that believes it is okay for another to pay for your problems, then you must understand that you are an enemy to the Constitution as you have just violated the idea that we are equals. What gives anyone the right to take from one to give to either themselves or another without just compensation?

Yes, there is a problem at hand but the good news is that we can change it without resorting to such ideas. Perhaps it starts with creating a way to penalize those who file frivolous lawsuits along with the attorneys involved if the lawsuit is found to be frivolous. If we are going to enact laws, why do we not enact some type of law that would fine those who abuse the systems provided? People might become less apt to follow through with such abuses for fear of the system coming back on them. Better yet, why not completely overhaul or rid ourselves of these illegal systems altogether?

The next step would surely be to teach our children the horrible repercussions of not being responsible for their actions. Essentially, when we put our livelihoods in the hands of another, we have given up our powers and freedoms, at which point, you are at the mercy of another.

This chapter has provided many different things to consider, but I would like to clarify the point. Nothing is free, not even your freedom. Nothing should be free. Entitlements are not a good thing. Socialized programs are not a good thing. Someone always has to pay somewhere. By subscribing to the idea of socialized or free, you are subscribing to the ultimate decay and destruction of the very principles this nation was founded on. Those who subscribe to such ideas should be regarded as enemies of the Constitution and as enemies of our founders.

Further Study

Recommended Books:

- Bad Leadership: What It Is, How It Happens, Why It Matters
  (Leadership for the Common Good) by Barbara Kellerman
- the deliberate dumbing down of america — A
  Chronological Paper Trail by Charlotte Iserbyt-Thomson
- The Liber t y Amendments: Restoring the American
  Republic by Mark R. Levin
- The School Revolution: A New Answer for Our Broken
- Education System by Ron Paul
- The Revolution: A Manifesto by Ron Paul
- The Case for Gold by Ron Paul and Lewis Lehrman
- The Fair Tax Book: Saying Goodbye to the Income Tax and
  the IRS by Neal Boortz and John Linder
- FairTax: The Truth: Answering the Critics by Neal Boortz,
  John Linder and Rob Woodall
- The Road to Serfdom by Friedrich A. von Hayek

Books with perspectives that surprise:

- Unintended Consequences by John Ross and T. J. Mullin
- Atlas Shrugged by Ayn Rand and Leonard Peikoff
- Age of Reason by Thomas Paine
- The Naked Communist by W. Cleon Skousen

Recommended Videos on Youtube:

- The American Dream (Animated)
- The Story of Your Enslavement

- Mind blowing speech by Robert Welch in 1958 predicting Insiders plans to destroy America
- Century of Self

Our Websites:

- www.AnAmericanWarning.com
- www.Facebook.com/AnAmericanWarning
- www.Youtube.com/AnAmericanWarningTV

If you haven't read it yet…

- Destroying the Narrative – Looking into the Gray

Fuzzy History

Get your facts straight.

By 1779, as many as one in seven Americans in Washington's army were black! The all-black First Rhode Island Regiment— composed of 33 freedmen and 92 slaves who were promised freedom if they served until the end of the war—distinguished itself in the Battle of Newport. Later, they were all but wiped out in a British attack.

When it comes to all deaths for children between the ages 0-14, 0.1% are from firearms, 0.6% is from motor vehicles, 5.3% are from being struck in beatings or bludgeoning, 6.0% from poisoning, and 42.6% from suffocation.

Did you know that our 32nd president of the United States Franklin D. Roosevelt was related, either by blood or by marriage, to 11 former presidents? Talk about keeping the power within the family.

Approximately 25 million American adults are living with their parents.

More people have been diagnosed with mental disorders in the United States than in any other nation on earth.

In 1951, President Dwight Eisenhower signed an executive order making Jesus Christ the first American.

In 1974, the Vice President of the United States Spiro S. Agnew resigned due to allegations of partisanship.

Today, the United States puts a higher percentage of its population in prison than any other nation on earth does.

More than 20,000 men were killed, wounded, or missing in action in the battle of Antietam, September 17, 1862. This was the bloodiest one-day fight during the Civil War.

Where did the buffalo go? Nowhere! Today, more buffalo roam on the prairies of the American Midwest than before the Civil War. In Oklahoma they are considered pests.

Bombs, guns, war . . . is it all so bad? Ceiling fans cause more finger and lower arm amputations each year than all the wars in the world combined.

In 1770, Crispus Attucks whose father was African and whose mother was a Nantucket Indian became the first casualty of the American Revolution when he was shot in what would later be known as the Boston Massacre.

90% of all violent crimes in the US do not involve a gun of any type

World War II: The first German serviceman killed was killed by the Japanese (China, 1937); the first American serviceman to die was killed by the Russians (Finland 1940).

"Allah Akbar, Allah Akbar, La Allah Il Allah, La Allah Il Allah U Mohammed Rassul Allah" is heard by more people than any other sound of the human voice. This is the prayer recited by

muezzins from each of the four corners of the prayer tower as Moslems all over the world face toward Mecca and kneel at sunset. It means: *"God is great. There is no God but God, and Mohammed is the prophet of God."*

Up until December of 1941, the top US Navy command was called CINCUS (pronounced *"sink us"*), the shoulder patch of the US Army's 45th Infantry Division was the Swastika, and Hitler's private train was named *"Amerika."* In light of the war and similarities, all three names were soon changed for PR purposes.

World War II: Attempting an ambitious attack on the Japanese, a massive naval bombardment led the way for 35,000 US and Canadian troops to storm ashore Kiska, (an island in the Rat Islands group of the Aleutian Islands of Alaska). Twenty-one troops were killed in the firefight though they estimated that the casualties would have been astronomical had they actually confronted any Japanese on the island.

One of the holiest Christian holidays is named after a pagan goddess. The name *"Easter"* derives from the Anglo-Saxon goddess Eostre, who governed the vernal equinox. Oddly enough, during the equinox the sun also ends its cycle then resurrects three days later.

The courts have consistently ruled that the police do not have an obligation to protect individuals, only the public in general. For example, in Warren v. D.C. the court stated *"courts have without exception concluded that when a municipality or other governmental entity undertakes to furnish police services, it assumes a duty only to the public at large and not to individual members of the community."*

During the US Civil war, 200,000 blacks served in the Union Army; 38,000 gave their lives; 22 won the Medal of Honor.

Hitler was responsible for the deaths of between 5 and 6 million of Europe's Jews. An additional 6 million 'unwanted' people were also executed, including more than half of Poland's educated populace. That is a total of roughly 10 to 11 million of Europe's own people killed at the hands of Hitler. Stalin was responsible for the deaths of roughly 20 million of his own people in much the same manner. All of these un-natural deaths were the results of life in camps, of famine, executions, etc.

Before Russia was an Ally of the US, it was first an Axis Power up until Hitler decided to invade.

Martha Washington is the only woman whose portrait has ever appeared on a US currency note. Her portrait was on the face of the $1 silver certificate issues of 1886 and 1891, and on the back of the $1 silver certificate of 1896. Sacagawea and Susan B. Anthony are the only women pictured on a US coin. Both were honored on a dollar coin.

The only repealed amendment to the US Constitution deals with the prohibition of alcohol.

Approximately 48 percent of all Americans are currently either considered to be "*low income*" or are living in poverty.

Jimmy Carter was the first US president to have been born in a hospital.

Yasser Arafat won the Nobel Peace prize.

In 1938, Time Magazine chose Adolf Hitler for man of the year.

The most common name in the world is Mohammed

Expecting the worst? The Eisenhower interstate system requires that one mile in every five must be straight. These straight sections are usable as airstrips in times of war or other emergencies.

As many as 561 times a day, women use guns to protect themselves against sexual assault.

There are more unemployed workers in the United States than there are people living in the entire nation of Greece.

The United States has never lost a war in which mules were used

Today, over 80% of all toys are manufactured in China and other foreign sources that have demonstrated a poor track record of quality control and safety.

Benjamin Franklin was Americas first Postmaster General

The 2nd president of the United States (John Adams) and 3rd president of the United States (Thomas Jefferson) both died within just a few hours apart of each other on the same exact day of July 4th 1826. They are the only two presidents to die on the same day of the same year.

Adolf Hitler's mother seriously considered aborting him during her pregnancy, but her doctor talked her out of it.

The US Library of Congress is the world's largest library

Twelve people have walked on the moon.

Andrew Jackson was the only American president to have once been a prisoner of war

Aaron Burr conspired to detach the Western states and the Louisiana Purchase from the United States and create his own empire.

Dick Cheney and Barack Obama are eighth cousins.

As an innocent bystander, you are 5.5 times more likely to be accidentally shot by a police officer than by an armed civilian.

The only state in the U.S that grows coffee beans is Hawaii.

The active ingredient in most toothpaste is called sodium fluoride. Sodium fluoride can be lethal

In the United States, the Internal Revenue Service has an employee's handbook for the collections division unit that instructs employees on how to collect taxes after a nuclear war.

Breast fed babies score slightly higher on mental development tests than ones on formula.

66 percent of all Americans are considered to be overweight.

In the United States, one out of every four children is on food stamps.

The United States has the highest divorce rate on the planet.

It took from the founding of the nation until 1981 for the US national debt to cross the one trillion dollar mark. Today, we add more than a trillion dollars to our debt every single year.

Acknowledgements

First and foremost, I want to thank our Founding Fathers. Although we have pretty much destroyed everything you stood for, without you, we wouldn't have anything to destroy. Many of you devoted your lives to this "*experiment*" and many of you gave your lives seeing it through. Thank you does not say enough, but I am truly thankful.

I want to thank the patriots who have put their necks out on the line to publish information and distribute information such as what can be found in this book. I hope that the remaining Patriots will recommend such literature to masses.

I want to thank my daughter, Heather, for giving me the inspiration necessary to write this book and continue on the path in pursuit of liberty. You are literally every reason I have to continue fighting as I understand what I will be leaving you with. You are the reason I try to make a difference in this crazy world. My hope is that you understand that there is nothing in this world I love more than you and that I will continue to try and make this a better world for you to live in.

I want to thank my parents. Thank you for giving me the guidance, the love, and understanding and the discipline.

I would like to thank everyone involved with the FairTax. You had a dream and are working your butts off to achieve it. Thank you for your time, your money, your effort, and your guts on trying to accomplish something many believed (and some still do) couldn't be done.

I would like to thank every author, every radio show talk host, and anyone who has ever done research or written or even spoken about these subjects. Your exercise of your First Amendment right is what is allowing the rest of us to keep this dream alive.

I would like to thank anyone who has picked up this book. I hope you share it with everyone you know and even some you don't. I would also like to encourage you to write about some of the things in this book. Use the information and get it out into the people's hands. It is in fact up to us. Only we can make the change.

This book is now a part of the historical record. I would like to acknowledge those who are reading this many years from today. By the time you read this, many of my projections will have already come to pass. You will undoubtedly be able to see where I was right or where I was wrong. I hope you pick up the torch of liberty and run with it having learned from these words, but also the words of the Founders. Liberty is the key. Don't let our struggles go to waste.

To everyone, never stop educating yourself. Seek out the truth. Even if you disagree with some or everything I've written here . . . make sure it's for the right reasons. Make sure they are educated reasons. I don't expect everyone to agree with me or to draw the same conclusions. I'm glad not everyone does. But we have to be educated about it. Once again . . . thank you! Now . . . go warn others.

The Declaration of Independence.

In CONGRESS, July 4, 1776.

The unanimous Declaration of the thirteen united States of America,

When in the Course of human events, it becomes necessary for one people to dissolve the political bands which have connected them with another, and to assume among the powers of the earth, the separate and equal station to which the Laws of Nature and of Nature's God entitle them, a decent respect to the opinions of mankind requires that they should declare the causes which impel them to the separation.

We hold these truths to be self-evident, that all men are created equal, that they are endowed by their Creator with certain unalienable Rights that among these are Life, Liberty and the pursuit of Happiness. (Note: the original hand-written text ended on the phrase *"the pursuit of property"* rather than *"the pursuit of Happiness"* but the phrase was changed in subsequent copies in part because it was broader. The latter phrase is used today).

That to secure these rights, Governments are instituted among Men, deriving their just powers from the consent of the governed, That whenever any Form of Government becomes destructive of these ends, it is the Right of the People to alter or to abolish it, and to institute new Government, laying its foundation on such principles and organizing its powers in such form, as to them shall seem most likely to effect their Safety and Happiness. Prudence, indeed, will dictate that Governments long established should not be changed for light and transient causes; and accordingly all experience hath shown, that mankind are more disposed to suffer, while evils are sufferable, than to right themselves by abolishing the forms to which they are accustomed. But when a long train of abuses and usurpations, pursuing invariably the same Object evinces a design to reduce them under absolute Despotism, it is their right, it is their duty, to throw off such Government, and to provide new Guards for their future security.

Such has been the patient sufferance of these Colonies; and such is now the necessity which constrains them to alter their former Systems of Government. The history of the present King of Great Britain is a history of repeated injuries and usurpations, all having in direct object the establishment of an absolute Tyranny over these States. To prove this, let Facts be submitted to a candid world.

He has refused his Assent to Laws, the most wholesome and necessary for the public good.

He has forbidden his Governors to pass Laws of immediate and pressing importance, unless suspended in their operation till his Assent should be obtained; and when so suspended, he has utterly neglected to attend to them.

He has refused to pass other Laws for the accommodation of large districts of people, unless those people would relinquish the right of Representation in the Legislature, a right inestimable to them and formidable to tyrants only.

He has called together legislative bodies at places unusual, uncomfortable, and distant from the depository of their Public Records, for the sole purpose of fatiguing them into compliance with his measures.

He has dissolved Representative Houses repeatedly, for opposing with manly firmness of his invasions on the rights of the people.

He has refused for a long time, after such dissolutions, to cause others to be elected, whereby the Legislative Powers, incapable of Annihilation, have returned to the People at large for their exercise; the State remaining in the meantime exposed to all the dangers of invasion from without, and convulsions within.

He has endeavored to prevent the population of these States; for that purpose obstructing the Laws for Naturalization of Foreigners; refusing to pass others to encourage their migrations hither, and raising the conditions of new Appropriations of Lands.

He has obstructed the Administration of Justice by refusing his Assent to Laws for establishing Judiciary Powers.

He has made Judges dependent on his Will alone for the tenure of their offices, and the amount and payment of their salaries.

He has erected a multitude of New Offices, and sent hither swarms of Officers to harass our people and eat out their substance.

He has kept among us, in times of peace, Standing Armies without the Consent of our legislatures.

He has affected to render the Military independent of and superior to the Civil Power.

He has combined with others to subject us to a jurisdiction foreign to our constitution, and unacknowledged by our laws; giving his Assent to their Acts of pretended Legislation:

For quartering large bodies of armed troops among us:

For protecting them, by a mock Trial from punishment for any Murders which they should commit on the Inhabitants of these States:

For cutting off our Trade with all parts of the world:

For imposing Taxes on us without our Consent:

For depriving us in many cases, of the benefit of Trial by Jury: For transporting us beyond Seas to be tried for pretended offences:

For abolishing the free System of English Laws in a neighboring Province, establishing therein an arbitrary government, and enlarging its Boundaries so as to render it at once an example and fit instrument for introducing the same absolute rule into these Colonies

For taking away our Charters, abolishing our most valuable Laws and altering fundamentally the Forms of our Governments:

For suspending our own Legislatures and declaring themselves invested with power to legislate for us in all cases whatsoever.

He has abdicated Government here, by declaring us out of his Protection and waging War against us.

He has plundered our seas, ravaged our coasts, burnt our towns, and destroyed the lives of our people.

He is at this time transporting large Armies of foreign Mercenaries to complete the works of death, desolation, and tyranny, already begun with circumstances of Cruelty & Perfidy scarcely paralleled in the most barbarous ages, and totally unworthy the Head of a civilized nation.

He has constrained our fellow Citizens taken Captive on the high Seas to bear Arms against their Country, to become the executioners of their friends and Brethren, or to fall themselves by their Hands.

He has excited domestic insurrections amongst us, and has endeavored to bring on the inhabitants of our frontiers, the merciless Indian Savages whose known rule of warfare is an undistinguished destruction of all ages, sexes and conditions.

In every stage of these Oppressions We have petitioned for Redress in the most humble terms: Our repeated Petitions have been answered only by repeated injury. A Prince, whose character is thus marked by every act which may define a Tyrant, is unfit to be the ruler of a free people.

Nor have we been wanting in attentions to our British brethren. We have warned them from time to time of attempts by their legislature to extend an unwarrantable jurisdiction over us. We have reminded them of the circumstances of our emigration and settlement here. We have appealed to their native justice and magnanimity, and we have conjured them by the ties of our common kindred to disavow these usurpations, which would inevitably interrupt our connections and correspondence. They too have been deaf to the voice of justice and of consanguinity. We must, therefore, acquiesce in the necessity, which denounces our Separation, and hold them, as we hold the rest of mankind, Enemies in War, in Peace Friends.

We, therefore, the Representatives of the united States of America, in General Congress, Assembled, appealing to the Supreme Judge of the world for the rectitude of our intentions, do, in the Name, and by Authority of the good People of these Colonies, solemnly publish and declare, That these united Colonies are, and of Right ought to be Free and Independent States; that they are Absolved from all Allegiance to the British Crown, and that all political connection between them and the State of Great Britain, is and ought to be totally dissolved; and that as Free and Independent States, they have full Power to levy War, conclude Peace, contract Alliances, establish Commerce, and to do all other Acts and Things which Independent States may of right do. And for the support of this Declaration, with a firm reliance on the protection of divine Providence, we mutually pledge to each other our Lives, our Fortunes and our sacred Honor.

- New Hampshire: Josiah Bartlett, William Whipple, Matthew Thornton
- Massachusetts: Samuel Adams, John Adams, John Hancock, Robert Treat Paine, Elbridge Gerry
- Rhode Island: Stephen Hopkins, William Ellery
- Connecticut: Roger Sherman, Samuel Huntington, William Williams, Oliver Wolcott
- New York: William Floyd, Philip Livingston, Francis Lewis, Lewis Morris
- New Jersey: Richard Stockton, John Witherspoon, Francis Hopkinson, John Hart, Abraham Clark
- Pennsylvania: Robert Morris, Benjamin Rush, Benjamin Franklin, John Morton, George Clymer, James Smith, George Taylor, James Wilson, George Ross
- Delaware: George Read, Caesar Rodney, Thomas McKean
- Maryland: Samuel Chase, William Paca, Thomas Stone, Charles Carroll of Carrollton
- Virginia: George Wythe, Richard Henry Lee, Thomas Jefferson, Benjamin Harrison, Thomas Nelson, Jr., Francis Lightfoot Lee, Carter Braxton
- North Carolina: William Hooper, Joseph Hewes, John Penn
- South Carolina: Edward Rutledge, Thomas Heyward, Jr., Thomas Lynch, Jr., Arthur Middleton
- Georgia: Button Gwinnett, Lyman Hall, George Walton

A Personal Note from David

If you enjoyed this book, please take a moment to leave a review on Amazon. You would be amazed at how much a good review can influence others into exploring something they otherwise would not.

Also, if you have the means, be sure to help spread this information by sharing or buying this book for someone else. Remember: if the information stops with you, we accomplish nothing.

Hopefully now you can walk away from this book with an appreciation and better understanding of the facts and be willing to start uniting with others who seek REAL freedom, knowledge and Constitutional integrity.

Thanks for your efforts and support! Be sure to check out some of my other titles on the following page.

About the Author

David Robertson is a proud father, a son, and a brother. He is a researcher, a writer, public speaker and more. His passions include health, history, theology, politics and leadership.

A life-long student of many disciplines; David holds a Master's of Science in Leadership, graduated summa cum laude with a Bachelor of Science in both Security Management and Leadership and also holds educational certificates in Operational Leadership and Homeland Security; Active Shooter Scenario Trainer, among several others.

Be sure to check out some of his other titles such as:

- Reasoned Leadership

- Natural Health Made Easy: *The Briobiotic Protocol*

- Destroying the Narrative: *Looking into the Gray*

- Reason, Religion and the Trinion Contradictions

Bibliography

Agee, C. (2013). Professor Teaches all Whites are Racist. *The Western Center for Journalism* , http://www.westernjournalism.com/professor-teaches-whites-racist/.

American-Heritage. (2003). steal. *The American Heritage® Dictionary of the English Language, Fourth Edition.* , Retrieved September 9 2013 from http://www.thefreedictionary.com/steal.

Androcles. (400+B.C.). Androcles, son of Theodorus: on Tyranny. *Culture and Crisis in the Golden Age of Athens - Bret Mulligan 2009* , http://iris.haverford.edu/athens/2009/12/13/androcles-son-of-theodorus/.

Army. (2008). The atomic bombings of hiroshima and nagasaki. *Manhattan Engineer District of the United States Army.* , http://avalon.law.yale.edu/20th_century/mp10.asp .

Barnhill-Tichenor Debate on Socialism. (1914). *The National Rip-Saw No. 101* , pp. Pamphlet B262 .B3 1914 - 63 pp - http://debs.indstate.edu/b262b3_1914.pdf.

Bateman, L. C. (2013). It's Time to Talk About Guns and the Supreme Court. *Esquire* , http://www.esquire.com/blogs/politics/bateman-on-guns-120313.

Bear (Merriam-Webster.com n.d.).

(1909). Sec. 1. That the militia...shall be divided into two classes...the organized militia, to be known as the National Guard...and the remainder to be known as the Reserve Militia. In C. A. Beard, *Readings in American Government and Politics* (p. 308). Macmillan.

Benko, R. (2013, March 11). *1.6 Billion Rounds Of Ammo For Homeland Security? It's Time For A National Conversation*. Retrieved 2013, from Forbes: http://www.forbes.com/sites/ralphbenko/2013/03/11/1-6-billion-rounds-of-ammo-for-homeland-security-its-time-for-a-national-conversation/

Bennetts, M. (2013). Russian lawmaker wants to outlaw U.S. dollar, calls it a Ponzi scheme. *The Washington Times* , http://www.washingtontimes.com/news/2013/nov/13/bill-would-outlaw-us-dollar-russia/.

Besta, S. (2010, November 24). China, Russia to dump US dollar for bilateral trade. *International Business Times* .

Biography (Director). (2004). *Mahatma Gandhi: Pilgrim of Peace* [Motion Picture].

Black, J. N. (1994). *When nations die: Ten warning signs of a culture in crisis.* Wheaton, Ill: Tyndale House.

Blacks and the Democratic Party. (2008, April 18). Retrieved 2013, from Factcheck.org: http://www.factcheck.org/2008/04/blacks-and-the-democratic-party/

BLS. (2013). Labor Force Statistics from the Current Population Survey. *U.S. Bureau of Labor Statistics* , http://data.bls.gov/timeseries/LNS14000000.

Bondurant, J. (n.d.). Gandhi, mohandas karamchand. *scholastic.com* , http://teacher.scholastic.com/scholasticnews/indepth/upfront/grolier/gandhi.ht m.

Britannica. (2013). geoengineering. *Encyclopædia Britannica* , http://www.britannica.com/EBchecked/topic/1527153/geoengineering.

Brown, K. (2002). Project h.o.p.e. *Justice.gov* , http://www.justice.gov/usao/als/rei.html - (AUSTIN. (2011, Apr 6). Historical inaccuracies. Retrieved from http://www.economist.com/blogs/democracyinamerica/2011/04/historical_inacc uracies?page=1).

Burns, C., Barton, K., & Kerby, S. (2012). The state of diversity in today's workforce. *Center for American Progress* , http://www.americanprogress.org/issues/labor/report/2012/07/12/11938/the-state-of-diversity-in-todays-workforce/.

Cao, B., & Chen, J. (2009). China Needs U.S. Guarantees for Treasuries, Yu Says. *Bloomberg* , http://www.bloomberg.com/apps/news?pid=newsarchive&sid=a_dsDz145J_A.

Carrol, C. (2011). Socialism on the rise under Obama. *The Examiner* , http://washingtonexaminer.com/article/1033496.

Census. (2013). Trade in Goods with China. *US Census* , http://www.census.gov/foreign-trade/balance/c5700.html.

Census, U. (2011). *SIPP.* Washington D.C.: United States Census Bureau.

Cheng, D. (2013). Pentagon Report on China Reveals Comprehensive Military Buildup, Extensive Espionage. *The Foundry* , http://blog.heritage.org/2013/05/09/dod-china-report-reveals-comprehensive-military-buildup-espionage/.

Clark, G. W. (2007, March 5). Seven Countries In Five Years. (A. Goodman, Interviewer)

Collins. (2003). Private property. *thefreedictionary.com* , http://www.thefreedictionary.com/private property .

communism (oxforddictionaries.com n.d.).

Corsi, J. R. (2013). Here's the real unemployment rate. *WND* , http://www.wnd.com/2013/08/heres-the-real-unemployment-rate-2/.

CSPOA. (2013). Growing List of Sheriffs, Associations and Police Chiefs Saying 'NO' to Obama Gun Control. *CSPOA.org* , http://cspoa.org/sheriffs-gun-rights/.

Davis, S. (2012). This Congress could be least productive since 1947. *USAToday* , http://usatoday30.usatoday.com/news/washington/story/2012-08-14/unproductive-congress-not-passing-bills/57060096/1.

Democracy (Merriam-Webster.com n.d.).

DHS. (2013). The Office for State and Local Law Enforcement. *Official website of the Department of Homeland Security* .

Diamond, D. (2013). Why The 'Real' Unemployment Rate Is Higher Than You Think. *Forbes* , http://www.forbes.com/sites/dandiamond/2013/07/05/why-the-real-unemployment-rate-is-higher-than-you-think/.

Dictionary.com. (2013). Redistribution. *Dictionary.com* , http://dictionary.reference.com/browse/redistribution.

Ditcham, B. G. (2004). Review of Zuckerman, Larry, The Rape of Belgium: The Untold Story of World War I. *H-War, H-Net Reviews* , http://www.h-net.org/reviews/showrev.php?id=10090 .

DOD. (1962). "Justification for US Military Intervention in Cuba (TS)". *U.S. Department of Defense* , The Operation Northwoods document in PDF format on the website of the independent, non-governmental research institute the National Security Archive at the George Washington University Gelman Library, Washington, D.C.

DOD. (1962). *Memorandum for the Secretary of Defense.*
http://www2.gwu.edu/~nsarchiv/news/20010430/doc1.pdf: Department of
Defense.

Eliovits, N. (2013). The Coming End Of Quantitative Easing And The Ensuing Market
Correction . *Seeking Alpha* .

Emmit, L. (2011). Black Gold Grab. *RT News* ,
http://www.thepeoplesvoice.org/TPV3/Videos.php/2011/05/08/gaddafi-gold-for-
oil-dollar-doom-plans-b.

EO13406. (2006). Executive Order 13406. *Federal Register* , Vol. 71, No. 124.

Evergreen. (2013). Evergreen Supertanker. *Evergreen* ,
http://www.evergreenaviation.com/supertanker/mkts.html.

EWG. (2009). *National Drinking Water Database.* Washington, DC: Environmental
Working Group.

Failure to obey order or regulation, 10 USC § 892 - Art. 92. (Cornell University Law
School).

Farah, J. (2010). Experts: Mystery contrail was from Chinese missile. *WND* ,
http://www.wnd.com/2010/11/230425/.

FBI. (2013, October). FBI Chemical Industry Outreach Workshop . (Robertson,
Interviewer)

Filip, J. (2010). Your Ultimate Cheat Sheet To Unemployment Numbers. *Wall St Cheet
Sheets* , http://wallstcheatsheet.com/economy/your-ultimate-guide-to-
unemployment-numbers.html/.

Fletcher, M. A. (2013, October). Most Americans accumulating debt faster than they're
saving for retirement. *The Washington Post* .

FRB. (2013, October 9). *Federal Open Market Committee.* Retrieved October 10, 2013,
from Board of Governors of the Federal Reserve System:
http://www.federalreserve.gov/newsevents/press/monetary/20131009a.htm

FRB. (2013 , August 2). *Who owns the Federal Reserve?* Retrieved October 10, 2013, from
Board of Governors of the Federal Reserve System:
http://www.federalreserve.gov/faqs/about_14986.htm

Gandhi, M. K. (1928). *Satyagraha in South Africa.* Ahmedabad: original publisher: Navajivan Publishing House - online version by Dr. Vidula Mhaiskar.

Gandhi, M. (2002). *The essential gandhi: An anthology of his writings on his life, work, and ideas.* New York, NY: Random House LLC.

Gandhi, M. (1929). Young India. March 21.

GAO. (2007). Numerous Federal Networks Used to Support Homeland Security Need to Be Better Coordinated with Key State and Local Information-Sharing Initiatives. *GAO-07-455* .

Gertz, B. (2013). China Tests High-Speed Precision-Guided Torpedo. *The Washington Free Beacon* , http://freebeacon.com/china-tests-high-speed-precision-guided-torpedo/.

GoldSea. (2013). China Retaliates Against US Naval Presence with Ships in Hawaiian Waters. *GoldSea - Asian American News* , http://goldsea.com/Text/index.php?id=14775.

Halper, D. (2013). U.S. Spent $3.7 Trillion on Welfare Over Last 5 Years. *The Weekly Standard* .

Heriot, G. (2013). The sad irony of affirmative action. *National Affairs* , http://www.nationalaffairs.com/publications/detail/the-sad-irony-of-affirmative-action.

Heritage. (2013). Is There Really A Shortage Of Oil? *The Heritage Foundation* , https://www.askheritage.org/is-there-really-a-shortage-of-oil/.

Hickman, G. R. (1998). *Leading organizations: Perspectives for a new era.* Thousand Oaks, Calif: Sage Publications.

History.com. (1916). Pancho Villa raids U.S. *History.com* , http://www.history.com/this-day-in-history/pancho-villa-raids-us.

Hoft, J. (2010). "Missile" Fired Off California Coast On Same Day That Chinese Sub Surprised US Carrier Group. *Gateway Pundit* , http://www.thegatewaypundit.com/2010/11/missile-fired-off-california-coast-on-same-day-that-chinese-sub-appeared-in-us-carrier-group/.

Hosenball, M. (2013). New York case offers insight into secret war against Somali militants. *Reuters* , http://www.reuters.com/article/2013/10/06/us-usa-shabaab-rendition-idUSBRE9950HX20131006.

Hoyas, C., & Morrison, K. (2003, June 5). Iraq returns to international oil market. *Financial Times* , pp. http://ftmdaily.com/wp-content/uploads/2012/03/ft_iraq-returns-to-international-oil-market.pdf.

Huckabee, M. (2010). Facts and the fair tax. *mikehuckabee.com* , http://www.mikehuckabee.com/mike-huckabee-news?ID=f6d178a8-ffe3-4757-ab2b-33b4f246d7c0.

Hudson, A., & Lake, E. (2009). Napolitano stands by controversial report. *The Washington Times* , http://www.washingtontimes.com/news/2009/apr/16/napolitano-stands-rightwing-extremism/?page=all.

HuffPost. (2013, November 9). Boston Tea Party Was Act Of Terrorism? Texas Public Schools Teaching New History Lesson. *Huffington Post* , pp. http://www.huffingtonpost.com/2012/11/26/boston-tea-party-was-act-_n_2193916.html.

ignorant (merriam-webster.com n.d.).

Infringed (Merriam-Webster.com n.d.).

ISOM v. STATE, No. S91A0781. 408 S.E.2d 701 (1991) 261 Ga. 596 - Reconsideration Denied October 18, 1991. (Supreme Court of Georgia September 26, 1991).

Jackson, G. P. (2012). Russian Nuclear Bombers Intercepted Over West Coast on Fourth of July. *A Time For Choosing* , http://thespeechatimeforchoosing.wordpress.com/2012/07/07/russian-nuclear-bombers-intercepted-over-west-coast-on-fourth-of-july/.

Jackson, J., & Gutknecht, D. (2001). *Mahatma gandhi.* Hartwick Classic Leadership Cases.

Jefferson, T. (1787, December 20). Papers 12:440.

Jones (Director). (2001). *9/11* [Motion Picture].

Jones, N. (2013). *Fiat Currency.* Retrieved 2013, from Daily Reckoning: http://dailyreckoning.com/fiat-currency/

Kadlec, C. (2012). The Federal Reserve's Explicit Goal: Devalue The Dollar 33%. *Forbes.com* .

Kellerman, B. (2004). Bad Leadership. In Barbara, *Bad Leadership* (p. 120). Boston: Harvard Business School Press.

Kelo V. New London, (04-108) 545 U.S. 469 (268 Conn. 1, 843 A. 2d 500, affirmed Supreme Court June 23, 2005).

Kurland, R. (2012). Frequently asked questions about affirmative action. *American for a Fair Chance* , http://www.civilrights.org/equal-opportunity/fact-sheets/fact_sheet_packet.pdf.

LaFree, G. (2012). *Hot Spots of Terrorism and Other Crimes in the United States, 1970 to 2008.* College Park, MD: National Consortium for the Study of Terrorism and Responses to Terrorism.

Landler, M. (2013). U.S. Pushes for Global Eye on South Sudan Conflict. *The New York Times* , http://www.nytimes.com/2013/07/30/us/us-pushes-for-global-eye-on-south-sudan-conflict.html?_r=0.

Laurent, D. (Spring 2001). Kent State – A history lesson that he teaches and lives – Dean Kahler disabled during 1970 student demonstration at Kent State University. *Accent on Living* .

Lengyel, C. G. (2007). Department of Defense Energy Strategy. *The Brookings Institution* , http://www.brookings.edu/~/media/research/files/papers/2007/8/defense%20lengyel/lengyel20070815.pdf.

Lewis, D. (2011). When The Nazis Invaded America. *Now I Know* , http://nowiknow.com/when-the-nazis-invaded-america/.

Luke, J. (2011). The Misunderstood National Debt. *EconProph* , http://econproph.com/2011/03/02/the-misunderstood-national-debt/.

Lynch, C. (2013). Is the U.S. Ramping Up a Secret War in Somalia? *Foreign Policy* , http://www.foreignpolicy.com/articles/2013/07/22/is_the_us_ramping_up_a_secret_war_in_somalia_al_shabab.

Manager, P. (2006, August 26). Information Sharing Environment. . (S. g. Share", Interviewer)

Maryland, U. o. (2013). *National Consortium for the Study of Terrorism and Responses to Terrorism.* College Pa: DHS Science and Technology Center of Excellence.

McGough, S. (2013, January 15). *Department of Homeland Security: Sport rifle (AR-15) "suitable for personal defense" (Updates).* Retrieved October 2013, from Radio Vice Online: http://radioviceonline.com/department-of-homeland-security-sport-rifle-ar-15-suitable-for-personal-defense/

McHenry, J. (1906). Papers of Dr. James McHenry on the Federal Convention of 1787. *The American Historical Review 11 (3)* , 595-624 .

McQuaid, H. (2013). Law Professor Calls For Repealing 2nd Amendment, Leaving Gun Rights Up To States. *CTNewsJunkie* , http://www.ctnewsjunkie.com/ctnj.php/archives/entry/law_professor_calls_for_repealing_2nd_amendment_leaving_gun_rights_up_to_st/.

Merriam-Webster. (n.d.). Inflation. *Merriam-Webster.com* .

Merriam-Webster. (n.d.). Oppressive. *Merriam-Webster.com* .

Merriam-Webster. (n.d.). Tyranny. *Merriam-Webster.com* .

militia (merriam-webster.com n.d.).

Morgan, D. (2013, October 2). Massive Debt Problem. (G. H. USAWatchdog.com, Interviewer)

Mulligan, C. B. (2010). In a first, women surpass men on u.s. payrolls. *The New York Times* , http://economix.blogs.nytimes.com/2010/02/05/in-historical-first-women-outnumber-men-on-us-payrolls/?_r=0 .

Murse, T. (2013). How Much U.S. Debt Does China Really Own? *US Government Info* , http://usgovinfo.about.com/od/moneymatters/ss/How-Much-US-Debt-Does-China-Own.htm.

NCES. (2013). *Literacy, Numeracy, and Problem Solving in Technology-Rich Environments Among U.S. Adults.* Washington DC: National Center for Education Statistics.

Newman, J. J., & Schmalbach, J. M. (1998). *United States history : preparing for the advanced placement examination.* New York, N.Y: Amsco School Publications.

Nickelodeon (Director). (2002). *Spare A Dime* [Motion Picture].

Oaths of enlistment and oaths of office. (2011, June 14). Retrieved from Center for Military History: http://www.history.army.mil/html/faq/oaths.html

Obama, B. H. (2013, September 18). Remarks by the President at the Business Roundtable. (T. W. House, Interviewer)

OECD. (2013). *OECD Skills Outlook 2013: First Results from the Survey of Adult Skills*. OECD Publishing.

Olson, M. (2002). *Power and prosperity: Outgrowing communist and capitalist dictatorships*. New York, N.Y: Basic Books.

Osborn, A. (2008). As if Things Weren't Bad Enough, Russian Professor Predicts End of U.S. *The Wall Street Journal*, http://online.wsj.com/news/articles/SB123051100709638419.

Ove, T. (2008). An american face to the tragedy of hiroshima. *Post Gazette*, http://www.post-gazette.com/stories/local/region/an-american-face-to-the-tragedy-of-hiroshima-406448/ .

PANNA. (2010). Silver iodide. *PAN Pesticides Database* .

PBS (Director). (2002). *The Rise and Fall of Jim Crow* [Motion Picture].

Petrodollar. (2013). Petrodollars. *Investopedia*, http://www.investopedia.com/terms/p/petrodollars.asp.

Pilon, M. (2009). The Buying Power of a Dollar, on a Downswing. *Wall Street Journal* .

Poverty Programs Create Welfare Addiction. (2011, June 01). Retrieved 2013, from Newsmax: http://www.newsmax.com/Stossel/minimumwage-LBJ-waronpoverty-povertylevel/2011/06/01/id/398412

Prive, T. (2012). Top 10 Qualities That Make A Great Leader. *Forbes*, http://www.forbes.com/sites/tanyaprive/2012/12/19/top-10-qualities-that-make-a-great-leader/.

Putin, V. (2009). Putin Speaks at Davos. *The WallStreet Journal*, http://online.wsj.com/news/articles/SB123317069332125243.

Rand, A. (1996). *Atlas Shrugged*. New York: Signet.

Rawles, J. (2012). Beware of Homeland Security Training for Local Law Enforcement. *Survivor Blog* , http://www.survivalblog.com/2011/03/beware_of_homeland_security_tr.html.

Republic (Merriam-Webster.com. n.d.).

Reuters. (2000). U.N. to let Iraq sell oil for euros, not dollars. *CNN.com* , http://edition.cnn.com/2000/WORLD/meast/10/30/iraq.un.euro.reut/.

RIANovosti. (2006). Russian bombers flew undetected across Arctic - AF commander. *RIA Novosti* , http://en.ria.ru/russia/20060422/46792049.html.

Rippey, D. R. (2001). Confucius, Machiaveeli, and Rousseau: Studies in Contrast . *Hartwick classic leadership cases* .

Roberts, D. (2009, May 19). China and Brazil: Dump the Dollar. *Bloomberg* .

Rogers, J. (2008, April 15). Jim Rogers: China's Economic Advance is All But Unstoppable. (M. Morning, Interviewer)

RT. (2011). Saving the world economy from Gaddafi. *RT News* , http://rt.com/news/economy-oil-gold-libya/.

Schmidt, & Hans. (1987). Maverick Marine: General Smedley D. Butler and the Contradictions of American Military History. In *ISBN 978-0-8131-0957-2 (paper)* (pp. 218-219). U. Press of Kentucky.

Snyder, M. (2013, May 16). 10 Amazing Charts That Demonstrate The Slow, Agonizing Death Of The American Worker. (T. E. Collapse, Interviewer)

socialism (oxforddictionaries.com n.d.).

socialism (oxforddictionaries.com n.d.).

Starnes, T. (2013). Pentagon training manual: white males have unfair advantages. *FoxNews* , http://www.foxnews.com/opinion/2013/10/31/pentagon-training-manual-white-males-have-unfair-advantages/.

Strategic-Essentials. (2010). Discover the best method of motivation. *Leadership Management Institute* , JOURNAL, VI(2).

Sunshine, M. (2013). Experts Agree The Fed's In Big Trouble. *Forbes* .

Sutton, B. (2011, Oct 25). "Every day in the United States, we are losing 15 factories.".
(PolitiFact, Interviewer)

Treasury. (2013). MAJOR FOREIGN HOLDERS OF TREASURY SECURITIES. *Treasury.gov* ,
http://www.treasury.gov/resource-center/data-chart-
center/tic/Documents/mfh.txt.

Types of Law Enforcement Agencies. (2013). Retrieved 2013, from Dicoverpolicing.org:
http://discoverpolicing.org/whats_like/?fa=types_jobs

Tyson, C. (2011). *Ameroca's New World Order: A Global Atlantis for the Age of Aquarius.*
Mustang: Tate Pub & Enterprises Llc.

Tytler. (1834). *Universal History – From the Creation of the World to the Beginning of the
18th Century.* Boston: Fetridge and Company (1850).

U.S. Declaration of Independence (1776).

U.S.Chamber. (2013). U.S. Chamber Releases Report on Chinese Investment in U.S.
Infrastructure. *U.S. Chamber of Commerce* ,
http://www.uschamber.com/press/releases/2013/october/us-chamber-releases-
report-chinese-investment-us-infrastructure.

US Const., art. IV, § 4.

US Const..

US-History. (2013). The development of the bureaucracy. *Independence Hall Association*
, http://www.ushistory.org/gov/8a.asp.

USIC. (2013). The US Inflation Calculator uses the latest US government CPI data
published on Sept. 17, 2013 to adjust for inflation and calculate the cumulative
inflation rate. *US Inflation Calculator* .

Valiente, A. (2012). Qatar's Petro Dollars Spent to Recruit, Train Terrorists in Lebanon to
Join War on Syria . *Syria 360°* , http://syria360.wordpress.com/2012/10/28/qatars-
petro-dollars-recruit-train-terrorists-in-lebanon-for-war-against-syria/.

Villarreal, R. (2013, March 26). So Long, Yankees! China And Brazil Ditch US Dollar In
Trade Deal Before BRICS Summit. *International Business Times* .

Watson, F. (2013). *Let Me Finish People Thoughts and Opinion: The Good, the Bad, the
Hateful.* Xlibris Corp.

Williams, J. (2013). Alternate Unemployment Charts. *Shadow Government Statistics* , http://www.shadowstats.com/alternate_data/unemployment-charts.

Williams, J. (2013, Oct 16). Early Stages of Hyperinflation Next Year. (G. H. USAWatchdog.com, Interviewer)

Williams, R. (2013). CIA backs $630,000 study into how to control global weather through geoengineering . *The Independent* , http://www.independent.co.uk/news/world/americas/cia-backs-630000-study-into-how-to-control-global-weather-through-geoengineering-8724501.html.

Willie, D. J. (2013, October 6). Systems are Breaking in Treasury Bond Market. (G. H. USAWatchdog.com, Interviewer)

Wong, J. (2006). A better way to tax. *The Tech - Online Edition, Feb 21* , 126(5).

Xinhua. (2013). U.S. fiscal failure warrants a de-Americanized world. *Xinhuanet.com* , http://news.xinhuanet.com/english/indepth/2013-10/13/c_132794246.htm.

Yu, M. (2013). Inside China: Nuclear submarines capable of widespread attack on U.S. *The Washington Times* , http://www.washingtontimes.com/news/2013/oct/31/inside-china-nuclear-submarines-capable-of-widespr/?page=all.

89987754R00208

Made in the USA
Middletown, DE
19 September 2018